Assessing Quality
in European Higher Education Institutions

Chiara Orsingher
Editor

Assessing Quality in European Higher Education Institutions

Dissemination, Methods
and Procedures

With 13 Figures
and 8 Tables

Physica-Verlag
A Springer Company

Chiara Orsingher
Associate Professor of Marketing

University of Bologna
Department of Management
Via Capo di Lucca, 34
40126 Bologna
Italy
E-mail: chiara.orsingher@unibo.it

ISBN-10 3-7908-1659-0 Physica-Verlag Heidelberg New York
ISBN-13 978-3-7908-1659-4 Physica-Verlag Heidelberg New York

Cataloging-in-Publication Data applied for
Library of Congress Control Number: 2005935313

Physica is a part of Springer Science+Business Media

springeronline.com

© Physica-Verlag Heidelberg 2006
Printed in Germany

Cover Design: Erich Kirchner
Production: Helmut Petri
Printing: Strauss Offsetdruck

SPIN 11562894   88/3153 – 5 4 3 2 1 0 – Printed on acid-free paper

Table of Contents

Introduction

Chiara Orsingher

University of Bologna, Italy

Attention is increasingly being focused on quality management in higher education institutions throughout Europe. The reasons lie with some relevant political and social changes happened in the last few years. Firstly, a large number of education institutions all over Europe have seen a progressive withdrawal of the State as the main financing body of the university system. Higher education institutions were therefore compelled to try and develop new ways to attract students and financial resources. Secondly, after granting higher education institutional autonomy, the State has required more transparency and accountability. Thirdly, a series of external factors, such as the labour market, the European higher education arena and the increasing social relevance of research and higher education led universities to the implementation of quality assurance procedures.

In light of these new challenges, quality assurance represents for many higher education institutions the main tool for planning, managing and controlling their own activities. Transparency, accountability, legitimacy of degrees and comparability between different European higher education institutions are just some of the achievements of the quality assurance process.

In Europe, the meaning of quality assurance is being developed in apparently different ways. In some countries quality assurance is an internal responsibility of each higher education institution and is based on an internal evaluation of the institution's programmes. In other countries, quality assurance entails an external evaluation or accreditation. In the first case, external peers evaluate programmes and institutions, while, in the second case, an external independent agency grants a specific 'quality label' to programmes and institutions which have met a set of pre-defined requirements.

This difference in terms of tradition and meaning allocated to the idea of quality assurance represents, on the one hand, a hindrance to the integration process of European higher educations, which is also hoped for by the Bologna Declaration. On the other hand, these different approaches might foster the development of a European quality assurance mechanism based, for instance, on the mutual acceptance of different systems.

This book offers a starting point for such reflection. It is a collection of case studies about different quality assurance procedures implemented in relevant higher education institutions of some European countries.

Before describing the contents of this book, it is now worth explaining the reasons which brought about it. The starting point was a research project funded by the Ministry for Education, University and Research and by the University of Bologna aimed at promoting the internationalisation of the university system and enhance the mobility among teachers and technical and administrative staff throughout European institutions. To this purpose, teachers and technical administrative staff of the University of Bologna visited some European higher education institutions. At the same time, a few foreign representatives experienced in evaluation and accreditation were invited to hold several lectures at the University of Bologna.

The tangible result of this project lies in this book which collects the evaluation and accreditation experiences gathered by higher education institutions in Finland, France, Germany, Italy, the Netherlands, the United Kingdom, Spain and Sweden. Every case study in this book features a recurrent pattern. To start with, information is provided about the quality assurance system of each country. Then, a specific higher education institution case study is introduced. In this part high premium is placed on the operating principles of the quality assurance system and on its impact on the organisation. This book does not aim at an exhaustive description of the quality assurance scenario either at European level or at national level. However, a few lessons for a future European dimension of quality assurance can be drawn from a cross-reading of the case studies presented.

Finally, this project also brings about an intangible result such as the relations and cultural exchange networks built up between the people who took part in this initiative. These networks do not only help standardize future quality assurance systems, but they can also act as the driving force for the development of cultural projects at European level.

Acknowledgements

I wish to acknowledge the support of the Italian Ministero dell'Istruzione, dell'Università e della Ricerca (MIUR) and of the University of Bologna for the grant that financially supported the project and the preparation of this book. In addition, I would like to thank the Rector of the University of Bologna, Professor Pier Ugo Calzolari, and the Administrative Director, Mrs. Ines Fabbro, for their encouragement during the early stages of the project. This book was made possible thanks to the time, efforts and the enthusiasm which all its contributors and the hosting universities devoted to the project. My warmest thanks go to them all. In particular, I would like to thank my colleagues Silvia Giannini and Muzio Gola for their co-operative attitude.

I should also like to thank Anna Maria Tironi, Catia Trombetti and Elisabetta Adinolfi for taking care of all the administrative details so efficiently. I would then like to thank Francesca Trombetti who contributed to this project with her experience.

Lastly, a special note of thanks goes to Laura Morigi, who supported me throughout the project with her competence, efficiency and kindness.

Quality assurance and evaluation of programmes at the University of Bologna

Daniela Darchini[1], Silvia Giannini[2], Muzio Gola[3]

University of Bologna, Torino Technical University, Italy

1 Introduction

With its 23 faculties, 68 departments and about 100,000 students enrolled, the Alma Mater Studiorum - University of Bologna is one of the largest higher education institutions in Italy. Since the early nineties it has been implementing a project of de-localization of its activities, opening four branches in the southern part of the region and one international centre in Buenos Aires.

In 1999 the Reform Law of universities ushered in a process of unprecedented change and innovation in Italian universities by means of two main cornerstones: the autonomy of universities and the adoption of the guidelines of the Bologna Declaration and subsequent acts [1]. The University of Bologna played a primary role in the implementation of the reform and today, five academic years later, it has fully implemented the new model, thus organising the whole teaching activity according to the "3+2" year scheme required by the reform.

The implementation of some of the most significant elements of the Bologna process in such a short period of time and with limited financial resources has been made possible by a joint effort by all sectors of the university community: students, technical and administrative staff and faculty members. In the spirit of the Bologna Declaration, the reform mainly focuses on five objectives:

- achievement of curricular flexibility;
- adoption of a mainly two cycle-system;
- introduction of a credit transfer system based on the ECTS (European Credit Transfer System)
- innovation in teaching programmes taking account of students' needs;

---

[1] Project Coordinator - University of Bologna
[2] Project Scientific Manager - University of Bologna
[3] Project Consultant – Torino Technical University

– increase system flexibility and its ability to renew itself.

Once this new model and the autonomy principle of universities were fully implemented, it was time to look ahead and deal with the issue of quality certification and accreditation of new curricula. For this reason an experimental project about "programmes quality certification and evaluation" was financed and launched in 2003. The aim was to test the implementation of such functions with particular reference to the European and international experience and debate on the subject. The final goal was to get ready to address the issue of quality enhancement along with quality certification and evaluation in compliance with the procedures already implemented in many other European higher education institutions.

2 Quality evaluation of higher education in Italy

2.1 The stakeholders

A number of institutions and bodies are in charge of or have a more general interest in the quality evaluation and accreditation process of degree courses. The most important institutions are:

- MIUR (www.miur.it), the Ministry of Education, University and Research (established in 1999 by the merger of the Ministry for Education and the Ministry for University and Scientific Research);
- CNVSU (www.cnvsu.it), the National Committee for the Evaluation of the University System, which is the institutional body in charge of general university evaluation criteria;
- CRUI (www.crui.it), an association made up of the Rectors of all Italian universities, raising the awareness of governmental and parliamentary authorities about the needs of the University system and supporting the university initiatives at national and international level;
- CNSU, the National Council of University Students, which is an advisory body made up of students' representatives;
- CUN, the National University Council, a representative body which promotes university autonomy and puts forward proposals about all major issues regarding university planning and administration.

The MIUR, along with its technical body - the CNVSU - is formally responsible for establishing quality evaluation and accreditation rules at the national level. Nonetheless, the other stakeholders, the CRUI in particular, significantly contributed to the debate about which system and which testing procedure for protocol evaluation should be implemented.

One of the most relevant activities was the nationwide Campus project (1995-2000) [3] in teaching processes evaluation which was organised and managed by the CRUI and funded by the European Union. The Campus project applied quality management procedures to almost a hundred university diploma programmes (approximately comparable to the present 3-year degree course prior to the reform), provided by twenty universities in Italy. Later initiatives followed the Campus experience, such as the SI.N.A.I. self-evaluation pilot project, which was promoted by the Conference of the Deans of the Engineering Faculties and involved a small number of engineering degree courses, and the Campus*One* project [4], which was launched by the CRUI as a direct follow-up of Campus for the academic years 2001-2004.

2.2 Regulatory framework

In Italy the Ministerial Decree 509/99 empowered each university to establish its own institutional teaching regulations, expressly stating that these regulations had to identify means for verifying or evaluating the quality of educational provision (Art. 11/indent 7-1).

Moreover, Annex 1 (Art. 4/4) to the ministerial Decree No. 115 (May 2001) states that each degree course must implement "an ongoing quality evaluation system for educational organisations and that the outcomes of degree course evaluations must meet national and international criteria". The Annex also states that degree courses must necessarily take into account "prospective employment opportunities and comply with the requirements of the outside world".

Subsequent ministerial documents clarified the purpose and scope of these new requirements. Accreditation procedures and criteria were set out in the MIUR-CNVSU Document 12/01 (July 2001) "Implementation of a course accreditation system in Italian universities: initial recommendations and proposals", which illustrated the structure of a document (called Quality Management "Information Model") whereby objectives, processes and intended outcomes of degree courses were stated.

The MIUR - CNVSU Document No. 17/01 (December 2001) about "minimum resources for university courses" put forward requirements for determining whether each degree course was run by a specified minimum number of faculty members and suggested that limits had to be set to the number of students enrolled in each degree course. These measures were to be immediately implemented. The document also stated that subject classifications would be re-examined in the nearest future and that checks on university facilities (e.g., classrooms, lecture halls, laboratories and libraries) used for specific programmes would be carried out at a later date.

The Ministerial Note No. 995 (July 2003) provided further details concerning minimum requirements and returned to the open issue of degree courses quality assurance: "until now the procedures for accrediting degree courses and their institutional structures have been developed at national and/or Community level in compliance with the objectives stated in the 1999 Bologna Declaration. It is therefore necessary to adopt a set of necessary structural and process parameters to ensure quality and provide students with a basis of comparison for making informed choices".

2.3 Definitions

The **Evaluation** of a programme or of an action (a degree programme, in our case), as stated in [5], is a cognitive activity that:

- allows to make an informed judgement about the degree course programme;
- is carried out according to clear, explicit procedures;
- is intended to have an impact on the degree course programme.

Evaluation is *formative,* if its purpose is to improve the programme or action, to organise the processes involved more effectively and to make adjustments on the way, when things do not seem to be working out. Formative evaluation is essentially based on qualitative judgements provided by experts, although it also relies on data and indicators. Evaluators generally conclude their work with recommendations, participate in the programme or action and share responsibility for it. For this type of evaluation, continuous monitoring and improvement are more important than the identification of the strengths of the degree programme.

Evaluation is *summative* when it is concerned with accountability, with certification and with the summing up of the entire programme or action. A summative evaluation heavily relies on data and indicators and it provides a final a judgement about the value of the programme (or action).

Accreditation has several meanings. In the strictest sense, it refers to *professional accreditation,* which is used to determine whether a programme or a qualification ensures access to a particular profession. More broadly, it refers to *academic accreditation,* which states that certain stated quality objectives have been met. Accreditation can also be seen as an extreme form of summative evaluation, although it differs from evaluation in that it returns a verdict which is either "yes" or "no", "pass" or "fail". Accreditation criteria state the principles higher education institutions must abide by and translate them into a set of qualitative or quantitative statements, which allow understanding how and to what extent these principles are complied with. Consequently, accreditation must be based on criteria or standards that are stated as clearly as possible. As previously mentioned, accreditation is often described as a public acknowledgement stating that a certain quality threshold has been met or exceeded. However, accreditation aims at achieving quality by simply ensuring that minimum standards are complied with.

2.4 Evaluation and accreditation features

Thus, degree programme evaluation and accreditation procedures must be viewed as part of an international process whose objective is to *describe, develop and certify competencies*.

What should then be evaluated?

– Internal efficiency or how smoothly the organisational machine is run?
– Economic efficiency?
– External effectiveness or to what extent the programme meets the needs it is required to fulfil?

Each one of these three options represents a distinct evaluation philosophy and the third one clearly ranks first. Identifying the learners' needs entails:

– identifying relevant objectives (i.e. *fitness of purpose* concept):

  • by drawing on contributions from stakeholders outside the university, the degree course programme must identify overall learning outcomes which will enable students to meet their further study and career aspirations;

– enabling the majority of students to achieve these objectives (i.e. *fitness for purpose* concept):

  • the degree course programme must allow students to gather useful learning experiences to achieve the stated objectives.

Such multifaceted needs cannot be met by simply relying on quantitative indicators that measure students' progress, performance or achievements. These indicators are certainly useful since they can condense large amounts of information in an objective form and point out any unusual feature. Indicators are therefore necessary since they help keeping the programme on track by avoiding pure idiosyncrasies, but they do not provide any information about actual the teaching and learning processes behind them.

Indicators must thus be accompanied by qualitative information about the factors that most contribute to creating an effective learning environment: faculty competence, the necessary commitment level of faculty members, how effectively the programme meets educational needs, whether adequate human and material resources are provided and whether the methods used for teaching and student assessment are effective.

It is important to make sure that the provision of this qualitative information is not seen as a bureaucratic chore, but as an indication of the fact that degree programmes can encourage faculty members to do their best.

Last but not least, accreditation encompasses many different concepts and has been implemented in many different ways. Similarly, any new approach to quality assurance and accreditation in the Italian system of higher education must be compared with previous experiences and the multitude of procedures that Italian universities have more or less systematically implemented over the years. Equally intense and extensive attention has been devoted by educators and legislators alike to the quality evaluation of the system. This is explicitly stated in the standards and guidelines for Quality assurance drafted by the European Network for Quality Assurance in Higher Education (ENQA, 2005) [2] and adopted by Ministries in the Bergen Communiqué.

Introducing an accreditation system that fails to build on the skills that Italy's higher education system and individual universities have acquired in this area would mean ignoring one of our most valuable assets and thus undermining the system's feasibility.

At the same time, a modicum of order and method should be brought to the many disparate approaches to internal/external quality assurance in use today, thus cutting the costs involved, optimising the effort and investments put into these programmes and making it easier to communicate and share experiences and best practices. A system is needed that does not impose hard and fast rules but establishes a common language and a set of clear and consistently applied mechanisms which ensure that higher education meets its objectives and its most basic aim, that is, serving the country and the public at large.

3 The "Project for Programme Accreditation" at the Alma Mater Studiorum - University of Bologna

3.1 General information

In September 2001 the University of Bologna saw the approval by the National Ministerial administration (MIUR) of 10 projects to support innovation in the educational process.

The aim of one of these projects (No.8), hereafter briefly named "Accreditation of Programmes", is to set up criteria for programme quality certification and evaluation bearing in mind the long-term possibility of European level accreditation.

The project stems from several initiatives already completed or currently underway at national and local level. The Campus project, the SI.N.A.I. and the Campus*One* project are the most significant activities carried out.

Starting from the experience gathered, project No. 8 established the following short-/medium-term objectives:

- spread the culture of quality;
- test self-evaluation and external evaluation processes in selected programmes at the University of Bologna;
- coordinate evaluation activities and other projects carried out on this subject at the University of Bologna;
- maintain relations with national boards and projects;

Project No. 8 also sets other more ambitious and long term objectives:

- extend the evaluation approach throughout the University of Bologna;
- prepare programme accreditation.

The project focuses on the new three-year programmes deriving from the implementation of the Bologna process, which was set up by the higher education reform introduced by act 509/99, and is currently in his third year. The following sections will describe the first two years by pointing out the approach followed and the most relevant outcomes.

The project has gone through different stages, each being characterised by the implementation of one of the evaluation/accreditation models available in Italy, carefully investigating their advantages and shortcomings from both a theoretical and practical viewpoint. During its first two-year period, which expired precisely while this paper was being written, the task forces participating in the project have tried to implement quality monitoring procedures following two approaches that will be described in the following section alongside related findings. The Scientific Manager and the Project Coordinator ensured project coordination and organised periodic review meetings. At present the project is coming to an end with a proposal for a model which aims at being the "best combination" of European experiences and the best compromise between completeness and sustainability.

The overall budget for the project approved by the administration board of the University is about 900,000 € and covers all expenses for the whole period 2003-2005.

3.2 Project Coordinator and Scientific Manager

The Scientific Manager was appointed among the professors of the University of Bologna that had experience in degree courses evaluation by having taken part in evaluation bodies and activities. The Scientific Manager is entrusted with the setting up of the activity framework for the project, mainly by means of presentations and discussions during project plenary meetings.

The Project Coordinator is an expert in quality assurance who periodically monitors project outcomes and establishes guidelines to make this outcomes as uniform as possible. He/she also runs a *project coordination office* that collects documents, builds relations among project participants, organise the logistics of plenary meetings and of the other project events.

3.3 Project Phase I (2003)

Before describing the project activities, it is now worth briefly introducing the boundaries and constraints that characterise the management of a study programme in Bologna and in Italian universities at large. Each degree course is ruled by the "Consiglio di Corso di Laurea (CCdL)", a board composed by all professors and some elected students' representatives. The President of the CCdL is responsible for steering CCdL's meetings and actions and for reporting about the CCdL's decisions. The CCdL usually entrusts the analysis and the proposal for solution of specific problems to *ad-hoc* "committees". The findings of these committees are then submitted to the CCdL that may decide whether to accept or not the proposals put forward.

It is therefore obvious that the CCdL, its President and, possibly, an *ad-hoc* committee are the primary subjects of any quality assurance activity regarding the study programme.

In the first stage the project coordination decided to continue the experience of the Campus project, adopting the new CampusOne model, which was introduced in 2002.

To perform the tasks envisaged by the evaluation model, both Campus and, later on, CampusOne require that each study Programme is equipped with a specific task force entrusted with the implementation of the self-evaluation document and its reporting to the CCdL. Such task force should include non-academic administrative staff, named Course Manager (CM), an academic manager, named Self-evaluation Professor (SeP), and a Programme Self-evaluation Board, which will include the President of the CCdL.

The programmes participating in the project were selected after informal talks between the Project Manager and the Faculties. The aim was to include staff members who were most keen to take part in such a project and start a self evaluation process, and, at the same time, have a sample of programmes representing at least most of the Faculties of the University of Bologna and therefore a large variety of taught subjects.

This last point is of great importance given the need to make sure that the self evaluation model was applied consistently throughout the University and not just in a specific subject area.

The project currently involves:

- 30 Degree Courses (listed in Tab.1), representing 8 Faculties and 4 locations (Bologna, Forlì, Cesena, Rimini);
- 16 Course Managers (CMs),
- 30 Self-evaluation professors (SePs),
- 1 Scientific Manager,
- 1 Coordinator

Table 1. The 30 degree course programmes involved in the project

Faculties	Degree courses
Medicine	Physiotherapy
	Nursing
Mathematical, Physical and Natural Sciences	Information Technology
	Internet Science
Mathematical, Physical and Natural Sciences (Cesena)	Information Sciences
Arts and Philosophy	DAMS-Drama, Art and Music Studies
	Geographical Sciences
	History
Advanced School of Modern Languages for Interpreters and Translators	Translation and Liaison Interpreting
Economics (Rimini)	Economics of Tourism
	Economy and Management of Tourist Services
	Economics and Business Administration
	Economics and Management
Engineering - Second Faculty (Cesena)	Biomedical Engineering
	Telecommunications Engineering
	Electronic Engineering
Engineering - Second Faculty (Forlì)	Mechanical Engineering
	Aerospace Engineering
Agriculture	Marketing and Economics of the Agro-industrial System
	Technologies of Vegetal Productions
	Protection of Plants and Vegetal Products
	Territorial and Agro-forestry Sciences
Agriculture (Cesena)	Food Sciences and Technologies
	Viticulture and Oenology
	Food Consumption and Catering Sciences
Veterinary Medicine	Aquaculture and Ichthyopathology
Economics (Forlì)	Economics of Co-operative Companies and Non-profit Organisations
Political Sciences (Forlì)	Sociology and Criminology Sciences for Safety
	Diplomatic and International Sciences
	Institutions, Economy and Policies of the European Union

3.3.1 Self-evaluation Professor (SeP) and Course Manager (CM) training

The SePs were chosen among the degree course staff members by giving priority to teachers that already had some knowledge, experience or had been involved in evaluation processes, or that were at least acquainted with the management of programme-specific processes.

The CM is considered within the Campus model as the coordinator of the different steps of the teaching process and he/she constantly monitors the process to make sure that quality standards are met. According to the CRUI, CMs should be recruited among University technical and administrative staff or even from the outside, but should have a higher education qualification, feature an extensive culture, good relational and team work skills and be highly motivated.

Some of the most frequent CMs activities should be:

- disseminate information and guide students;
- monitor processes;
- search information and classify data concerning resources;
- help the self-evaluator in drafting the self-evaluation report;
- interact with staff and organisations;
- adopt a quality-system based approach.

The task force needs some training before starting its job. As to the present project, training was provided by exploiting the experience gathered in the Campus and CampusOne projects, which was applied to some programmes of the University of Bologna since their beginning. The CRUI staff provided training for SePs and CMs with three short courses on Didactic Management for CMs and two courses on the CampusOne self-evaluation model for both SePs and CMs. This training was completed in the first few months of the project.

3.3.2 The deployment of Phase I

The CampusOne model is strongly inspired by ISO 9000:2000 standards. It identifies five key-dimensions, which are then further expanded in a set of basic elements for each dimension.

The model requires that the degree courses focus on and provide information about several elements, while still keeping an overview of the whole evaluation process.

The five dimensions and the related elements are reported below:

Dimension 1: **Organisation,** broken down under three elements:

- Management system
- Responsibility
- Review

Dimension 2: **Objectives, requirements,** broken down under three elements

- Requirements
- General objectives of the study programme
- Learning outcomes

Dimension 3: **Resources,** broken down under two elements:

- Staff
- Facilities

Dimension 4: **Teaching process,** broken down under three elements:

- Design of the programme
- Teaching provision
- Services

Dimension 5: **Results,** broken down under two elements:

- Results
- Analysis, improvement

The self-evaluation reports (SERs) were completed and delivered to the coordination office in December 2003. An external expert in self-evaluation and peer review of the CampusOne model was then invited to review the SERs and provide comments and tutoring on the task forces.

1. The SERs and their subsequent external review highlighted some weaknesses of the programmes, above all, the lack of a complete and well defined set of processes and a clear allocation of responsibilities. Moreover, the reporting of quantitative and qualitative information was not fully exploited to identify critical issues and suggest improvement strategies.

In addition to providing information on the quality, as well as the weaknesses, of each programme involved in the project, the implementation of the CampusOne/CRUI model during Phase I, highlighted some critical points, on which most SePs and CMs agreed: excessive attention devoted to processes, severe redundancies, use of technical-specific language, specialised character of the self-evaluation document which does not serve the purpose of public information.

Last but not least, the cost-benefit ratio of the whole process of producing and reviewing the SER was too high to be adopted throughout the University of Bologna in consideration of the large number of programmes potentially involved. The University of Bologna currently runs about 140 Degree Courses.

3.3 Phase II (2004)

On the basis of the Phase I experience, the activity of Phase II was planned with the major aim to solve the most important problems, with the following priorities:

- be more focused on results rather than on procedures;
- produce simple and readable documentation even for non-experts, in particular for the public and for the stakeholders, enabling them to come up with personal and verifiable judgements;
- have a better knowledge of the experience gathered at international level;
- better match the features of a complex and multifaceted institution such as the University of Bologna.

As a result, an evaluation model compliant with the above-mentioned criteria has been recently proposed by a Work Group set up by the CNVSU-MIUR and has been described in an official research report, although it has not been adopted by the Ministry as a viable tool yet [5].

This Work Group, which is coordinated by Prof. Muzio Gola of the Politecnico di Torino (Torino Technical University), concluded its work with a final report including the proposal for an "Information Model" or, better, an information protocol. Such protocol is extremely similar to the CampusOne checklist, but is considerably simpler and it points out the minimum quantitative and qualitative information needed to formulate an external opinion about the expected quality level of the programme learning outcomes.

3.3.1 Information model for degree course accreditation: Document RdR 1/04 MIUR-CNVSU

This "model" or protocol, hereafter referred to as the "RdR 1 / 04", takes into account the international debate about degree courses accreditation, international certification requirements, such as the ECTS label, production of the diploma supplement, the need to check course organisation with respect to a limited number of "key" actions that are necessary to evaluate a study programme for accreditation purposes. The last feature significantly reduces the amount of paperwork.

In order to produce a sustainable scheme, the RdR 1 / 04 proposes that the set of requirements and indicators and the supporting evidence must take the shape of a "synthesis" information document, as opposed to the current form of "analysis" reports. The preferred form is that of summary "Tables" to be filled in following common criteria, thus making comparisons much easier.

The quality of degree course programmes is to be ensured through documented control of four <u>key dimensions</u>:

1. External requirements and learning outcomes
2. Teaching, learning and assessment
3. Resources and services
4. Monitoring, analysis and review

To keep the amount of topics that must be covered by each dimension within manageable limits, but to ensure that no potentially accreditation-relevant aspect is overlooked, dimensions are divided into a uniform set of <u>factors</u>. The Work Group has identified the type of <u>evidence</u> that must be gathered in exploring these factors and the dimensions linked to them. Dimensions, basic factors and evidence are summarised in the following tables.

Table 2. Correspondence between dimensions / factors / evidence of the information model (source [5])

Dimensions	Factors	Evidences required
A Require- ments, objectives	Parties consulted to identify external (occupational/ professional/ educational) requirements; requirements identified: reference professional roles, competences needed to perform such roles; learning outcomes: knowledge and skills necessary for the development of competences[a].	Table A1: Consultation with socio-economic forces Table A2: Educational requirements Table A3: Learning outcomes and breakdown of Study programme under areas

Table 2. (cont.)

B Teaching, learning, assessment	Characteristics of students' enrolments structure and contents of Programme teaching methods and materials; learning assessment methods.	Tables B1a, B1b: Educational prerequisites (selection, orientation) Table B2: Study programme Table B3: Calendar of teaching activities Annex II: Course module data sheet
C Resources, services	Teachers and their competences; technical-administrative support; facilities (classrooms, laboratories, equipment, libraries …) tutoring, assistance and students' support.	Teachers' CV: hyper-textual link in Table B2 Table C1: Rooms
D Monitoring, analysis, review	Students' enrolments and progress data (internal effectiveness); opinions of students and graduates occupational outcome of graduates (external effectiveness); data analysis and comments; periodic review activities.	Table D1: Students enrolments and progress data (internal effectiveness); Other data to be defined (see Table D2)[b]; Students' opinions (attending and about to graduate) upon completion of CdS Data on occupational outcomes; Table D3: Course analysis, monitoring, review.

[a] The British QAA has developed the so-called "benchmarking statements" which are detailed statements of the attributes and characteristics that students must possess in order to be awarded a degree. The Tuning project has been developed through European cooperation among institutions 'reference points', 'level descriptors' and professional profiles described in terms of learning outcomes and subject specific and generic competences for several disciplinary areas. http://www.qaa.ac.uk/academicinfrastructure/benchmark/default.asp.

[b] Other data (to be defined) can be added to Table D2 in cooperation with the Anagrafe Nazionale degli Studenti (National Student Registry) by taking due account of the requirements associated with the Diploma Supplement.

3.4 Implementation of the "Information Model" and project costs

The work carried on during the first year with the contribution of the Project Consultant allowed to test the application of the MIUR/CNVSU model. Feedback was provided and some proposals for changes were put forward so that the model could be more easily understood and implemented. Moreover, it was possible to test the evaluation task force, with particular reference to the role of the SeP and CM, and to better define their tasks and activities. Up to now the experience gathered on the project has proven that this task force is necessary to properly support the evaluation process.

The final versions of the "Information Model" (or protocol) for the academic year 2004-2005 will be made available by the end of September 2005 and will be published on the project website [6].

In addition, the implementation of this project has entailed a series of other positive side-effects that should be briefly mentioned.

Firstly, links and coordinated activities have been created with other quality assurance projects within the University of Bologna (Interlink, Board for the Evaluation of Teaching, Tuning, Teep, CampusOne), in order to exchange information and discuss the outcomes of related experiences. Two Conferences on evaluation and quality assessment of teaching processes have been jointly organised (one of the two conferences has been organised in synergy with the activities supported by the European Commission for the promotion of the Bologna process).

Moreover, the need to provide the information required by the model in a satisfactory and well consolidated way stimulated interactions with the University Internet and information systems management departments which were encouraged to provide guidelines concerning information to be put on-line and Degree Courses. This is the requirement for achieving the ECTS label and providing the Diploma supplement. Talks are underway to ensure that these contents include all the information that is needed to fill in the models in the future.

To collect the necessary data a wide use has also been made of the new Data Warehouse and of other databases of the University. During the last decade, the University of Bologna made a big effort in automating all administrative processes by means of sophisticated information systems. Nowadays, all the information data related to the teaching activities as well as to university staff and funding are managed by means of specific, but interacting databases. In particular, a Data Warehouse has been recently developed in order to have a uniform, coherent and updated database including all students and their individual careers. Thanks to the close cooperation and interaction with the project "Accreditation of programmes", output formats of the Data Warehouse have currently been standardised in order to comply with the requirements of evaluation and accreditation models.

Last but not least, cooperation and coordinated activities are currently being started with other Universities that are also testing the same "Information Model".

4 Conclusion

In summary, although the project is still in progress, a number of important achievements can be pointed out. To start with, it was possible to better understand the degree of complexity and the effectiveness of the reporting required by the quality evaluation process while the project was underway.

The experience gathered during the first year, which was based on the implementation of the CampusOne model, was very useful to introduce the culture of quality assessment. At the same time, it also shed some light on some of the limits of the adopted model. As previously mentioned, the extension of this model to a complex institution, such as the University of Bologna, would have put an excessive burden on the model. More importantly, the model showed some inherent complexities that made it partially unsuitable to provide the necessary information to all the outside parties who are interested in the aims, methods and outcomes of degree courses.

Bearing in mind that there is no unique, well defined and readily available model for quality assessment, the new "Information Model" adopted in the second and third year of the project seems more capable to fulfil the major aims of a quality assurance process, since its widespread implementation is feasible and it can suitably provide public information. The model actually follows similar guidelines to the CampusOne model, but it is as simple as possible. At the same time it is transparent and it provides the minimum quantitative and qualitative information which is necessary to formulate an external opinion about the programme quality.

The lesson to be drawn from this experience is that, regardless of the model adopted, it is of vital importance that all teaching activities of the University are progressively involved in the quality assurance process as part of a coordinated strategy. The adopted model/models must then meet some basic principles and requirements, in order to ensure transparency, accountability and allow external evaluation. An "agreed upon set of standards, procedures and guidelines on quality assurance" has been recently developed by the ENQA, in cooperation with the European University Association (EUA), the European Association of Institutions in Higher Education (EURASHE) and the National Unions of Students in Europe (ESIB). These standards and guidelines have been adopted by the European Ministers in charge of Higher Education in the Communiqué of the Conference of Bergen, 19-20 May 2005. The "Information Model" implemented at the Bologna University complies with these guidelines and standards and could therefore contribute to the introduction and development of a systematic method for higher education quality assurance not only at local, but also at national level.

References

1. Bologna Declaration (19 June 1999) http://www.bologna-bergen2005.no
2. ENQA (European Network for Quality Assurance in Higher Education) Standards and Guidelines for Quality Assurance in the European Higher Education Area, Helsinki, Finland, 2005
3. http://www.campus.it
4. http://www.campusone.it
5. MIUR (Ministry of Education, Universities and Research), CNVSU (National Committee for the Evaluation of Higher Education): Information Model for Degree Programme Accreditation, Final Report of the Work Group on "Evaluation of Teaching and Accreditation"; RdR 1 / 04 February 2004. http://www.cnvsu.it
6. http://accreditamento.unibo.it

Quality assurance in United Kingdom higher education. A case study: the London Metropolitan University

Cinzia Castelluccio, Lanfranco Masotti[1]

University of Bologna, Italy

1 Introduction

The aim of this study is to present the Quality Assurance System of one of the largest universities in Great Britain, the London Metropolitan University (London Met). A brief history of the evaluation system in the United Kingdom (UK) and a description of the current situation of Higher Education in the UK, as to the quality and standard assurance will be presented to start with. In particular, we will describe the activities carried out by the national Quality Assurance Agency and the quality procedures implemented in England, Northern Ireland, Scotland and Wales.

As to the London Met, after a short presentation of the University, we will try to present an overview of the quality assurance and management systems, their facilities, the people involved (boards, committees, departments, internal and external examiners) and the procedures currently in place. Finally, we will describe the policy adopted by the London Met with respect to external accrediting agencies and professional bodies that also reported to the organisation of the QAA Institutional Audit in spring 2005.

---

[1] Acknowledgements: We acknowledge all the Direction and Staff of the London Metropolitan University for allowing us to visit their offices and departments and to exchange opinions and knowledge about the Quality Assurance System. A particular thank goes to Robert Aylett, Jill Grinstead and Trevor Joscelyne for their kind welcome and the excellent organisation of our visit. We also thank John Lally, Jan Dixon, Catherine Connor, Cornell Coggins and the staff of the Department of Art, Media and Design, of the Department of Health and Human Sciences and of the Department of Quality and Standards for dedicating some of their time to our meeting.

2 Brief history of the quality evaluation system in the United Kingdom

During the last twenty years, the transition of higher education from a system based on a small elite to a system based on mass participation has transformed the relationship between higher education and society [1]. In a small, elitist university system, academic standards and quality were implicit: the added-value brought about by higher education was clearly understood. In a mass participation system, standards and value must be made explicit to those investing time and money in study. New stakeholders come to the fore with new expectations and information needs to be met.

For this reason there is now a need for external quality and standards assurance. The transition to mass higher education is a phenomenon involving both developed and developing countries.

In most countries universities have to stand new pressures, such as the increasing number of students and the participation of private finance in higher education. They then also need to prove that quality standards are preserved and enhanced. To this purpose, many countries have set up national organisations to carry out an independent quality and standards evaluation in higher education institutions. In most cases, initiatives have been promoted by governments. The International Network of Quality Assurance Agencies in Higher Education currently has affiliates in 47 countries throughout the world.

3 Higher education institution in the United Kingdom: power and responsibilities

There are over 180 universities and colleges of higher education in the UK. They are autonomous, self-governing institutions, even though most of them are entirely funded by the government through higher education funding councils [2]. There are independent councils for England, Scotland and Wales.

Some of these institutions have the power to award degrees: since 1992 all the universities have been allocated this power by the Privy Council, upon the advice of Government.

Higher education institutions without a proper degree awarding power have to prepare their students for degrees awarded by authorised universities under a licensing or 'validation' arrangement.

At present, each higher education institution is responsible for the standards and quality of its academic awards and programmes. Each institution features its own internal procedure for attaining appropriate standards and assuring and enhancing the quality of the education provided. In particular, they consider two points: 1) students' assessment of students; 2) procedures for programme design, approval, monitoring and reviewing.

Most institutions both regularly monitor and periodically review programmes.

The monitoring activity evaluates how effective a programme is and how successful students are in meeting the learning outcomes. This activity is generally performed by the department providing the programme, usually at the end of an academic year. The monitoring process may also consider reports from external examiners, staff and student feedback or reports of any professional body that accredits the programme. The results obtained can determine some adjustments to the curriculum or to students' assessment procedures to ensure continued effectiveness.

The periodic review of institutions is normally carried out every five years and it usually involves external experts. It makes sure that the programme objectives are still valid and are being achieved by students. Institutions have made arrangements to conduct periodic reviews of the support services they make available to their students. Each higher education institution appoints external examiners who report to the head of institution. They are independent academic experts from other institutions or from other areas of relevant professional practice. They provide impartial advice on performance as regards specific programmes. External experts formulate judgements about the implementation of the standards set for the awards by referring to subject benchmark statements; higher education qualification and institutional programme specification frameworks; students' performance standards compared with similar programmes in other UK higher education institutions; assignment processes implemented by the institution for assessment, examination and determination of awards.

From 2004, all higher education institutions in England are required to make available information on: institutional context; students' admission and career progression; internal procedure to assure academic quality and standards.

Some of these data will be published on the Higher Education and Research Opportunities (HERO) web site at www.hero.ac.uk.

4 The assurance of standard and quality in higher education in the UK

In the UK *Teaching Quality Assessment* (TQA) was first introduced in 1993 and, prior to the setting up of a National Agency, was carried out separately by each of the Higher Education Funding Councils [3]. The analysis was conducted on a subject basis. The first subject reviews, which were originally carried out by the Higher Education Funding Council for England, covered all subject areas (such as Art, Media and Design, Education, Health and Human Science) taught in higher education institutions in a cycle lasting from 1993 to 2001.

The way in which judgements were reported varied within the UK and over time. In England and Northern Ireland, the TQA analysed students' learning experience and achievement from 1993 to 1995. Each subject area received a judgement ranging from "excellent", "satisfactory" and "unsatisfactory". From 1995 to 2001, universal subject reviews covered six aspects of provision (curriculum design, content and organisation; teaching, learning and assessment; student progression and achievement; student support and guidance; learning resources; quality assurance and enhancement). Each aspect was graded on a scale from 1 to 4, in ascending order of merit. The results of these reviews were published and each assessment was summarised by a "graded profile" or a "TQA score". Published TQA scores were used by some national newspapers in constructing "league tables" of higher education institutions. Of course, translations of descriptive profiles into a score could create limitations in making comparative judgements between the programmes and the institutions providing them.

In Scotland the TQA examined quality at subject level from 1993 to 1998 under five headings. Judgment was not based on numeric scores, as in England. During the last year of the review cycle a revised method of assessment was introduced, based on the six elements implemented by the English method.

Also Wales implemented an independent method to examine the quality of higher education provision from 1993 to 1998.

Moreover, from 1991 to 1997, the former Higher Education Quality Council and its predecessor, the Academic Audit Unit, conducted the first round of *Academic quality audits*. This was a form of enquiry covering all higher education institutions; its aim was to establish to what extent an institution could apply correct and effective procedures for standards and quality management.

After this cycle was completed, the subject review was due to be replaced by a new quality assurance method covering the entire provision throughout the United Kingdom.

In 1997, the *Quality Assurance Agency* (QAA) of higher education was established to provide an integrated quality assurance service for the UK higher education. From 1998 to 2002, a second round of Academic quality audits, known as continuation audits, was undertaken by the QAA. Continuation audit focused on quality strategy, academic standards, learning facilities and communications.

In 2003, the UK Government published its White Paper on "The Future of High Education": some of the proposals put forward in this paper will affect UK policy in this area.

5 The Quality Assurance Agency

In order to review standards and quality it is necessary to clearly define the following terms.

Academic standards describe the level of achievement that a student has to reach to gain an academic award (a degree, a master, etc.). It should be a similar level across the UK [1].

Academic quality indicates how effectively the learning opportunities made available to students help them in achieving their awards. This means checking that appropriate and effective teaching, support assessment and learning opportunities are provided.

In 1997, the *Quality Assurance Agency* (QAA) of higher education was established to provide an integrated quality assurance service for UK higher education. QAA is an independent body funded by the subscriptions of universities and higher education colleges and through contacts with the main higher education funding bodies. The QAA is governed by a Board, which is responsible for the strategic planning and direction of the Agency. The QAA's mission is to safeguard public interest as regards higher education and to ensure continuous improvement for quality management.

Each higher education institution is responsible for ensuring that appropriate standards are being achieved and that a high-level education is being offered. The QAA provides reference points that help to define clear and explicit standards. For each higher education institution, the QAA reviews standards and quality.

The QAA is a national institution, but there are different review systems in the different *countries*. In England and Northern Ireland, institutions are reviewed through an *institutional audit*. In addition, only in England and for a transitional period ending in 2005, institutions may also be reviewed through a *developmental engagement* or *an academic review at subject level.*

The *institutional audit* makes sure that institutions are providing higher education, awards and qualifications of acceptable quality and appropriate academic standards. Moreover, it ensures that universities exercise their legal power to award degrees in a proper manner.

The *developmental engagement* allows institutions to check their internal review procedure at discipline level or at programme level.

Academic review at subject level considers subject areas: in this case judgments are made on academic standards and the quality of learning opportunities for students. This last procedure is carried out in all English further education colleges that provide higher education programmes.

In Scotland, *enhancement-led institutional review (ELIR)* is an essential element of the new approach to managing quality and standards in Scottish higher education.

ELIR has been founded by the QAA in accord with Scotland Universities, student bodies in Scotland and the Scottish Higher Education Funding Council. ELIR analyses the methods used by each institution to continually raise awareness about students' learning experience.

In Wales, the purpose of *institutional review* is to check that the provision of higher education institutions is both of acceptable quality and compliant with appropriate academic standards. It also makes sure that the legal power to award degrees is being exercised in a proper manner. In the UK, the QAA conducts also overseas audits of partnerships between UK higher education institutions and organisations overseas that lead to the award of degrees from UK institutions.

The QAA resorts to review processes whereby teams of academics conduct audits and reviews. People from the industry and the profession can sometimes be involved.

The QAA helps to define clear and explicit standards for public information and acts as a reference point for its review activities. To this purpose, it has cooperated with the higher education sector and other stakeholders to implement the following initiatives.

The frameworks for higher education qualifications allow understanding higher education qualifications, by setting out the attributes and abilities that can be expected of a holder of a title, such as a bachelor's degree with honour, a master's degree and a doctorate. This way, they establish the meaning of a specific qualifications level and they also provide public assurance that qualifications bearing similar titles represent similar levels of achievement. A qualification framework is in place for England, Wales and Northern Ireland and one for Scotland, which is part of a wider Scottish Credit and Qualifications Framework.

Subject benchmark statements set out expectations about degree standards within a subject area range. They identify the defining features of a discipline, its identity and the techniques and skills which are necessary to develop an understanding of the subject. They also point out the level of intellectual demand and challenge a degree with honours requires in the subject area and support higher education institutions in designing and approving a programme.

Programme specifications are the information that each institution provides about its programmes. Each specification has to define what knowledge, skills and other attributes a student must achieve to successfully complete a specific programme.

In these specifications, institutions also define the teaching and learning method, the assessment and career opportunities and explain the relationship between programmes and the qualification frameworks.

Progress Files of students help to make the results of learning in higher education more explicit and more valuable: they contain the formal record of each student's learning and achievements, but also personal and development planning. This helps students to think about their own learning achievements and plan their education and career development.

The Code of practice for the assurance of academic quality and standards in higher education represents a guideline about the management of academic standards and quality. This code features ten sections and each of them contains principles institutions should comply with.

The QAA also carries out other activities. It advises Government on the allocation of degree awarding powers, university titles or designations for higher education institutions. It licenses Authorised Validating Agencies (AVAs) to recognise "Access to higher education courses" and issues certificates to be awarded to successful students. The QAA has established an "Access recognition scheme" to grant AVAs.

Moreover, the QAA is involved in international quality assurance initiatives: this includes membership of the International Network of Quality Assurance Agencies in Higher Education (INQAAHE) and the European Network for Quality Assurance (ENQA).

The QAA has developed a Strategic Plan 2003-05 [4] in which the Board of Directors has adopted a revised mission statement. These changes follow the rapid changes in the environment and in stakeholders' needs. Shortly before the publication of the Strategic Plan, the Secretary of State for Education and Skills published *The Future of High Education*. Some parts of this document are extremely relevant to the work of the QAA, such as the University title or the Access to Recognition Scheme, which the Agency offers in England, Wales and Northern Ireland. For this reason the QAA considers it extremely important to closely cooperate with the Government to ensure that all the changes are fully understood and that quality procedures are really implemented.

The Agency is in a transitional period: it has completed the planned review and audit programme established by previous bodies. During these years it has been developing and implementing new methods and it has played new and different roles across the UK.

6 A case study: the London Metropolitan University

The London Metropolitan University (London Met) is currently the largest single university in London and one of the largest in Britain. Given its location in one of the most exciting and challenging cities in the world, the London Met has strong links and closely cooperates with London's diverse communities, businesses, the industry and public institutions [5]. The teaching and research activities of the university are fully oriented towards the real needs of society and to promoting access to higher education in London, the southeast of England and across the world.

The London Met is situated in the City, in the north-east part of London, and it offers a wide variety of courses in a large number of subject areas. In particular, courses are planned in consultation with employers and examining bodies in commerce, industry, the world of art and design, financial services, industries and professions. Courses can be followed at several levels including, not only the undergraduate and postgraduate levels, but also other further education programmes, short courses and professional and institute qualifications. Many programmed courses can be followed either full or part time and the module scheme allows a flexible study programme.

The London Met is the major provider of business and vocational education of the City and the north-east part of London. This university promotes personal development through excellent and accessible education and training for those who work and live in London, or who wish to study in London, to meet the needs of its communities, professions, industries and trades.

Moreover, the education offered will equip students with cultural capital in addition to advanced subject knowledge and appropriate skills.

The London Met stimulates and assists the economic regeneration of the north-east of London and it can boast a year-long experience in dealing with the needs of mature and overseas students, playing a full and active role in the European as well as the wider international community.

7 Short presentation of the London Metropolitan University

The London Met was created on 1 August 2002 by the merger of London Guildhall University (now London City Campus) and the University of North London (now London North Campus): both institutions have their own histories behind them before being merged.

The London City Campus was founded over 150 years ago, in 1848, when the Bishop of London set up the Metropolitan Evening Classes for Young Men, to improve the moral, intellectual and spiritual condition of young men in the metropolis [6]. This became the City of London College over time. In 1970 the City of London Polytechnic was created by the merger of the City of London College, the Sir John Cass College and the King Edward VII Nautical College. In 1990 the London College of Furniture joined the City of London Polytechnic.

The London North Campus began its activity in 1896 as the Northern Polytechnic Institution, where not only English, mathematics and chemistry were taught, but also machine construction, plumbing, dressmaking and millinery. All subjects were taught at elementary level and most of them were offered as evening classes. However, this institution had an immediate success and in less than five years student numbers doubled.

In 1992 Further and Higher Education received Royal Assents: polytechnics were granted university status. The City of London Polytechnic became the London Guildhall University. The Polytechnic of North London became the University of North London. The merger was made in 2002 and it was the first merger between two universities in the UK.

The London Met has over 35,000 students and more than 3,300 academic and non –academic staff.

It offers over 240 undergraduate and 140 postgraduate courses and many more adult, pre-degree, industry training, professional and short courses.

The London Met has more than 7,000 international students of 188 different nationalities, from more than 150 countries outside the UK: this university has offices in Bangladesh, Brussels, China, India, Nigeria and Pakistan.

The London Met offers a very flexible modular course structure: it is possible to combine many subjects to obtain different degree programmes according to different needs and interests.

Moreover, study can be full-time, part-time, distance-learning, day and evening classes, starting in September or February.

In addition, the University offers access to learning facilities, such as libraries, learning centres, Information Technology (IT) laboratories and online reading facilities.

8 Academic regulations

The London Met has its own Academic Regulations [7]. The University's Academic Regulations represent the rules to be followed in order to attain university educational objectives. Academic Regulations govern the standards of the University's awards, the responsibilities of students and the formal roles played by staff as regards admission to university courses and programmes, assessment of students' work and granting of awards. They also govern the role of external examiners.

Academic Regulations establish processes and set out criteria for judging student academic performance. An essential purpose of these regulations is to ensure equity of treatment to students at each stage of their education. All students can gain the highest award for which, by means of their ability and dedication, they can qualify in the shortest time appropriate for them. Another purpose of these regulations is to protect the academic standing of the University and the academic integrity of its awards. These regulations also include university undergraduates and postgraduates courses. The regulation framework which governs these schemes complies with the Framework for Higher Education Qualifications in England, Wales and Northern Ireland. These schemes are based on a credit accumulation system compatible with others in the UK and in Europe. The scheme regulation framework and course regulations, which are approved on a regular basis on behalf of the Academic Board, shall comply with these Regulations.

As regards students, Academic Regulations do not only grant rights, but also responsibilities. They state that students have to attend classes and supervisory sessions, submit work for assessment, pay the established fees, but they also indicate how to comply with the administrative procedure. The London Met makes every effort to disseminate its Academic Regulations.

The Academic Regulations now in use are in compliance with university requirements for the maintenance of standards of its approved awards, including awards offered in cooperation with partner institutions or by distance-learning.

Academic Regulations are linked to the Quality Assurance Procedure: for example art. 2 of section B1.1 ('Generic principles for schemes and courses leading to university awards') of the Academic Regulation book 2003-04 states "All schemes and courses shall be approved, reviewed and modified in accordance with the Quality Assurance Procedure".

Academic Regulations represent the guidelines to be followed in order to govern a Higher Education institution. The London Met Academic Regulation Book 2003-04 is broken down under three different sections:

- A - Regulatory definition;
- B - Academic Regulations governing the standards of the University Awards, which includes the Generic principle for schemes and courses, the Undergraduate regulatory framework, the Postgraduate regulatory framework; the Research degree regulation, the Accreditation of prior (experiential) learning (AP(E)L) regulation, the London Met Awards Framework and the Regulation on assessment and certification;
- C - Regulations governing students' responsibilities.

9 The University's academic quality assurance system

The London Met complies with specific procedures to ensure that the academic standards of its awards are appropriate and that the quality of courses and services offered to students is as high as possible [8] [9].

The Academic Board is responsible for these quality assurance procedures, but the University's quality assurance system entrusts committees and individuals with specific responsibilities. Moreover, a quality control scheme is necessary to support the quality assurance system.

All quality procedures operate through the principle of peer review and will be implemented by taking into consideration the judgment of people involved in them.

Records and audit trails are published, so that the University can demonstrate the probity of its procedure.

The Department of Academic Quality, Standards and Policy Development supports academic departments for a correct application of quality procedures (see below).

Before analysing these procedures, quality assurance committees and boards must be introduced.

As already mentioned, specific committees and board are involved in quality assurance facilities and have different responsibilities. Some of them and their main roles are listed below.

The *Academic Board* exercises a primary role in quality assurance processes, although many of the operational aspects are then devolved to other committees. It analyses the reports of department reviews and subject level reviews. It also analyses reports on the outcomes of the overall annual monitoring activities. It is then responsible for several matters of academic policy and regulation relating to university courses. To this purpose it can receive advice from appropriate committees, such as the Academic Development Committee, the Quality and Standard Committee, the Research and Development Committee and the Information and Learning Committee. If the Academic Board has delegated its powers to its committees, it monitors their operation by requiring specific reports.

The *Academic Development Committee* has to advise the Academic Board on the development of the University's academic strategy. It is responsible for the development and the monitoring of policies and procedures for the operation of every type of academic provision. In particular, it approves proposals for new courses and for course closures; it receives information on quality assurance activities from the Quality and Standards Committee.

The *Quality and Standards Committee* is a central committee and is responsible towards the Academic Board for supervising the operation and the effectiveness of the University quality assurance procedures. It approves new courses and modifications to courses, according to the validation reports and review panels. Moreover, it has to indicate which members of the academic staff are judged to be qualified to participate in validation and review panels. The name of these members is noted in a specific register. It arranges and controls the activities of the departmental quality committee (or equivalent bodies). It monitors several other initiatives and it receives advice from appropriate groups. It receives advice, for instance, from the *Academic Audit Steering Group* in supervising matters connected with the QAA Institutional Audit and other reviews by external bodies.

The quality structure presents other additional group reports to the Quality and Standard Committee, the Accreditation of Prior (Experiential) Learning (AP(E)L) Board or the Research and Development Committee. Moreover, every department presents a Departmental Quality Committee or an equivalent committee, which should represent a link with the central structure.

According to the University's policy, each academic department is currently expected to set up a departmental Quality Committee, which will operate in compliance with specific references and responsibilities. However, each department can make its own decisions about this committee. Some departments prefer to combine quality matters with other related matters, such as teaching and learning activities In this case a department can propose a different committee from the standard Quality Committee. The proposal will be examined by the University Quality and Standards Committee and it will be accepted if the proposed committee has the same references and responsibilities of a standard Quality committee.

Furthermore, Departmental Quality Committees have to advise and assist the Head of Department on all department-related quality matters to manage and deliver the quality process according to the university's policy; to supervise the preparation of documentation to be submitted for department reviews which are carried out both internally within the University and externally by the QAA or professional bodies; to receive and recommend for approval proposals for modification and validation of courses or modules, if appropriate, before these are submitted to consideration, approval, validation or review, according to University quality procedure.

Moreover, these committees have to ensure that departmental academic information provided to students in course handbooks and other documentation is accurate, adequate and of appropriate quality. They have to report on departmental quality activities to the Quality and Standards Committee and are entrusted with the formulation, monitoring and review of departmental procedures as regards the communication with external examiners. They also have to recognise good practice within the department and record this in the annual monitoring procedure.

The Departmental Quality Committee or an equivalent body, even though not a standard one, must be able to maintain an objective position as regards quality matters and operate independently from the department executive management (Figure 1).

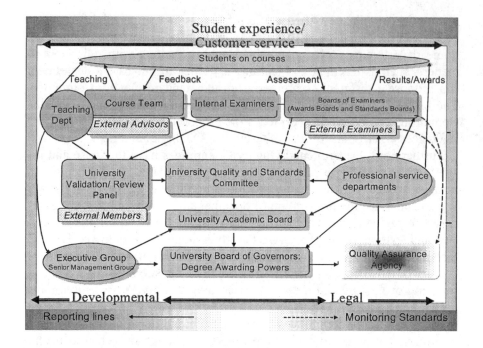

Fig. 1. The Quality Management Model (from Managing for Quality – a holistic model by Jill Grinstead)

10 The Department of academic quality, standards and policy development

All the University's quality assurance procedures are administered by this Department. This is a professional service department involving a staff of about thirty people [8] [9]. The Head of this department is the Director of Quality and Standards. The Department of Academic Quality consists of three units: the Quality Unit, the Academic Audit Unit and the Secretariat/Policy Coordination Unit. It also includes a *Partnerships office*, whose associate Director has responsibility for developing a major external partnership with the University.

The three units play distinctive roles in the University's quality assurance procedure.

The role of the *Quality Unit* is to promote and develop internal policy in relation to academic quality assurance. It cooperates with senior managers within the University and with the Chairs of the Quality and Standards Committee and Academic Development Committee. The Quality Unit has the responsibility to manage the central programme of validation and review activity. It advises university staff mainly the course leader, on the implementation of the University's policy and procedures for academic quality assurance.

Moreover, it administers the university procedures for the appointment of internal and external examiners and an officer of the Quality Unit supervises the work and provides advice for each validation and review panel.

The *Academic Audit Unit* provides administrative support for the agreements between the University and external agencies, such as the QAA and professional bodies. It also holds the electronic records of the University's courses and at the moment it is working to create a document management infrastructure which will comply with Teaching Quality Information requirements. The Academic Audit Unit works closely with academic departments to prepare subject-level reviews.

The *Secretariat/Policy Coordination Unit* provides policy and secretarial support for the University's central committees. In particular, the staff of this Unit closely cooperates with the Academic Board and is involved in the approval of course proposals. It also provides advice on regulatory matters within the University and is involved in the consideration of proposals for courses modifications (Figure 2).

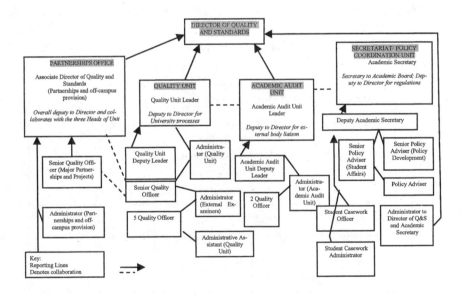

Fig. 2. Department of academic quality, standard and policy development

11 Quality assurance procedures

The information gathered by the Quality assurance system is reported in the "Quality Assurance Handbook", which was published by the London Met in September 2003. This Handbook is also very detailed in its explanations of the quality assurance procedures implemented by this institution [8] [10].

There are different quality assurance procedures (Figure 3) and most of them involve department planning and acts. Others relate to courses (outline approval, course validation, course modifications, annual monitoring); others are aimed at different department activities, such as the managerial health of the department with particular reference to the quality process and outcomes (*Department Review*). As to the standard model, the University is now going to move away from course-by-course review to introduce a *Subject-level Review*, which analyses the subject grouping of academic provision. However, there are still courses which, according to the University, need to be reviewed and the University has therefore retained its procedure for course review: if specific needs arise, the University can also perform periodic reviews.

The academic department is the "core" of the academic activity and all procedures concerning courses go through a system of departmental planning, in which proposals for new courses or course modifications are indicated.

Procedures concerning *Courses:*
• Outline approval (or Course closure)   • Course Validation   • Course Modifications   • Periodic Review   • Annual Monitoring
Procedures concerning   *Management of Quality and Strategic Planning:*   • Department Review   • Subject Level Review

Fig. 3. Quality assurance procedures

All quality assurance procedures feature a similar rationale, even though they are required to meet the specific aim of the procedure itself. A case in point is the department review.

All academic departments are submitted to the *Department Review* at the London Met. This is focused on departmental planning and management of services and resources, not on courses provision, which is analysed separately.

The department review analyses: departmental management and planning, quality management, arrangements for student support and guidance, management of student recruitment and career guidance, management and monitoring of resources, staff development and research, customer service, contact with other academic and professional service departments.

The aim of this analysis is to identify strengths and weaknesses in the department organization and to identify and disseminate good practices.

A department review (Figure 4) is provided to each department every three to six years and a schedule of the review is kept by the Quality Unit. The schedule is prepared by the Head of the Quality Unit in accordance with the Heads of Department and it is approved by the Academic Board.

The Quality Unit is entrusted with the organisation of an initial review planning meeting, in which the Secretary and the Chair of the review panel, the Head of the Department and the departmental staff indicated by the Head of the Department are involved. During this meeting, all details about the panel visit are established, such as date, timetable, review documentation, which the review panel needs to examine.

Each department to be reviewed has to produce a self-evaluation document (SED). The SED represents the centre of all documentation required for a department review. The content of the SED for department review is determined by each department, according to its particular structure and activity, but some guidelines are provided by the institution. As stated in Appendix 4 of the Quality Assurance Handbook "the guidance regarding the content and structure of documentation is therefore not intended to be prescriptive and departments should vary their inputs as necessary".

The SED must be prepared by using different department documentations, such as departmental plans, annual monitoring reports and also reports from other departments, such as the Systems and Services Departments. This document should not only be descriptive, but also evaluative and should report the sources on which department evaluations are based. Other descriptive documentation and also the quoted sources must be made available to the review panel before the visit.

The Head of the Department is responsible for the SED. Once it is prepared, the SED is approved by the Departmental Quality Committee and forwarded to the University Quality Unit. The deadline for the SED is established during the review planning meeting. The Quality Unit sends the SED to all the members of the review panel before the review event in order to facilitate the full analysis of the documentation. The panel members usually submit comments in advance to the department and the detailed agenda of the review is often based on this comments.

The review event usually lasts one day. During the visit the panel can meet department staff. At the same time, all documents quoted should be made available to the panel. Finally the panel reports its main conclusions to the department. In summary, at the end of the visit, the review panel formulates a peer judgment about the management of the department with particular reference to the quality process and its outcomes. The panel underlines the weaknesses and provides advice about any actions to be taken by the department or by the University to improve quality.

At the same time the panel identifies the good practices, which should be disseminated within the University. If further actions are recommended, the Head of Department has the responsibility to ensure that a report of the actions taken will be sent to the Quality and Standards Committee.

The review panel draws up a report, which is submitted to the Quality and Standard Committee. This Committee recommends the review to the Academic Board for approval. The Academic Board can refer back to review panel upon two situations: if the review panel does not comply with the correct procedure and if recommendations are inappropriate.

The approved review report and the comments of Quality and Standard Committee are made available to the Academic Development Committee, which is entrusted with academic planning.

At the end of each academic session the Quality and Standard Committee will prepare an overview of the entire review panel which has taken place during the session, to inform the Academic Board mainly about common themes or problems.

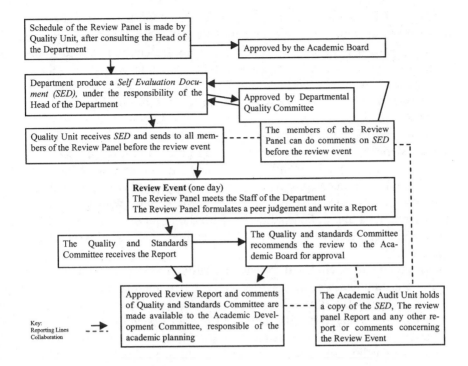

Fig. 4. An example of quality assurance procedure: department review

The Academic Audit Unit, one of the units of the Department of Quality, Standards and Policy Development, has the responsibility to keep a copy of the SED, the review panel report and any other reports or comments concerning the review event.

The Department Review procedure makes sure that each department is effectively managed, but, as previously stated, it does not analyse course provision.

As to this point, different procedures are implemented depending on whether a new course must be proposed and approved or a delivery of a validated course must be analysed.

For new courses the procedures of *Outline approval* and *Course Validation* must be met.

All the University's courses are subject to outline approval. New course proposals should be indicated in the departmental plans of each department 18 months in advance of the proposed start date, although courses can be planned in a shorter term in exceptional cases. The academic departments present course proposals to the Academic Secretary, which will be analysed by the Portfolio Development Group. This Group makes a recommendation for approval to the Academic Development Committee. A course proposal cannot be subject to validation, without a first clear outline approval. Once the course proposal is approved, it may be included in the University prospectus, as forming part of the academic provision "subject to validation". A similar procedure can be implemented for a proposal of course closure. The forms for these applications are provided by the Quality Unit.

All university courses are "subject of validation" before they may be offered to students. The University validation process ensures that courses meet the appropriate quality and standards and that courses, as well as their delivery and assessment procedures, are properly planned. Moreover the validation process makes sure that new courses comply with the University's regulations and policies and also with the requirements of the QAA Framework for Higher Education Qualifications and the QAA subject benchmarks.

This procedure includes different validation models: the Director of Quality and Standards decides which is the most suitable form of validation according to the type of course proposed. The Head of the Quality Unit receives extensive details about all the courses which have obtained outline approval and require validation. The Unit also supervises the appointment of validation panels. The department has to make sure that the course is successful although specific actions of the course leader, of the course development team and of the Head of Department may be required. The Head of Department has also to approve any course documentation which is submitted to validation.

Validation is a process whereby a validation panel analyses the course proposal, in order to evaluate if it has been designed according to University criteria.

Validation panels members are selected as follows: a minimum of two, but usually three members are selected from the University's register of "validators". One of the members is then designed to chair the panel. These members must not be part of the department which originally proposed the course. The Chair of the Quality and Standards Committee also selects three external advisors whose expertise is suitable to the course submitted for validation. One of them might have recent experience in an area or in a profession relevant to the course.

Before the validation event, the validation panel receives and examines all the documentation about the course. During the visit, the course development team and the course leader will jointly discuss about the documentation at the presence of the Head of the Department. At the end, if the validation panel considers the course appropriate, recommends to the Quality and Standards Committee that the course should be approved. No time limit is usually imposed for course approvals, although initial approval may be limited to a specified period in certain cases (for example in a rapidly developing field of study). All conditions of approval are reported to the Quality and Standard Committee, and, in some cases, also to the Academic Development Committee. The confirmed validation report is submitted to the Quality and Standards Committee, which usually approves it. The validation report is then sent to the host department and to other University staff, if necessary.

The course leader is responsible for the course handbook and for other related module booklets. The handbook is very useful for teaching staff and students. It describes the course structure and its regulations. For each course approved a course handbook is provided. An electronic copy of this handbook is sent by the course leader to the Quality Unit, when a new course is approved or whenever the course handbook or the booklets are modified, so that the central record of the University's courses is constantly updated. A copy of all the handbooks is lodged with the Academic Audit Unit, which is responsible for maintaining accurate course records.

The courses provided by the London Met University are subject to *annual monitoring*. This procedure is primarily implemented for the benefit of the department and its purpose is to check if modules and courses are being delivered in an effective way so that aims and learning outcomes are met and students can fully exploit their skills. Annual monitoring is retrospective, but it entails the introduction and the planning of changes to ensure a continuous improvement. Standardised reporting forms are provided and can be used for different kinds of courses and modules. The reports are analysed by the departmental Quality Committee. A member of the University Quality and Standards Committee is invited to attend the meeting of the departmental Quality Committee as an external peer. The departmental Quality Committee makes recommendations to the Head of the Department on the final approval of the course monitoring report. The Head of the Department takes responsibility for the annual monitoring of the academic provision within the department, by approving and signing the course monitoring reports and providing a monitoring overview, which is then submitted to the Quality Unit. The Quality and Standards Committee usually analyses the department overview report during its spring meeting and then reports the overall process to the Academic Board. Electronic copies of all the reports are held by the Academic Audit Unit. The annual monitoring process allows course leaders and departments to rethink about the courses provided. The London Met uses another procedure to analyse the courses provided by the University, which takes a broader and a more long-term perspective of the academic health and development of a subject grouping of courses. This procedure is the *Subject level Review* and is undertaken periodically. The purposes of this procedure are both to contribute to the University's central planning and to maintain and improve quality management at institution level. It is very useful to provide preparation for visits by external agencies, such as the QAA and professional bodies. In this case too, the Quality Unit is entrusted with organisation of the activities since it will group the provided courses in subject area, according to the academic departments. Each subject area will be reviewed usually every three to six years, following a schedule determined by the Quality Unit, after consultation with heads of academic department and subject leaders.

The subject review will be focused, among other things, on the overall development of the subject area and plans for future course developments/deletions in relation to external changes within the discipline; the impact of research and staff; student achievement across the subject area; feedback from professional bodies, subject review reports and any other external engagements; etc.

The subject level review follows almost the same procedure of the Department review procedure: details are reported on the Quality Assurance Agency Handbook.

In its quality assurance procedures the London Met has also introduced the *Appointment of examiners*. The London Met actually appoints qualified internal and external examiners to ensure that the standard of the University's awards is preserved. Moreover, they make sure that the assessment of students complies with this standard, so that all the students are evaluated by means of the same criteria.

The coordinator of the appointment and payment systems for examiners is a member of the Quality Unit staff. The regulation governing this role is included in the Academic Regulations.

The External Examiners for taught courses can perform two different roles: Subject Standards Examiners for module and Award Examiners for schemes and courses. The Head of Department, in agreement with the course leader, contacts an appropriate nominee and if he/she agrees, the Head submits his/her CV to the coordinator, who checks that the appointment is compliant with the University's regulations.

Afterwards, the nominee is submitted to the Examiners Group appointed by the Quality and Standards Committee. Each external examiner has to produce a report of his/her visit. The coordinator has to make sure that these reports are distributed. The contractual fee will be paid by University, only after the annual report has been received.

External Examiner appointments last normally for four years, but on request of the Head of Department, there will be an extension to five years.

Among External Examiners, there are members from professional bodies (i.e. member from the Law Society for Law Society courses).

In addition to External Examiners, the University appoints a number of internal examiners to become members of Award Boards and Subject Standards Boards. Chairs and Vice-Chairs are usually members of these Boards along with Module Internal Examiners. The appointment of these examiners is suggested by the competent Head of Department to the coordinator. All the Board members are appointed by the Examiners Group, which provides a recommendation to the Quality and Standard Committee.

12 Role of the students in quality assurance procedure

According to the national High Education practice, the London Met has established three different procedures to ensure the participation of students in the quality process:

1. questionnaires;
2. course committee;
3. student representation in University committees.

The London Met acknowledges the importance of student opinions at different levels and this element of the quality assurance framework could have great influence on the department's management and on course and module organisation.

In some cases, *focus groups* of students can be organised by departments, committees or course leaders to obtain students' opinion on specific matters in a shorter time.

As regards questionnaires, each module/course leader submits forms to students to obtain student feedback on learning and teaching activities. The questionnaires should be issued in a way as to get the maximum response. In addition to the basic questions connected to the relevant area, leaders can introduce further course/module related questions. Course and module leaders will collect the questionnaires and the results will be included into the annual monitoring report. The reports will be analysed by departmental Quality Committees.

Questionnaires are also prepared to evaluate learning resource areas, such as libraries or information technology facilities.

The course committee advises the Head of Department, course leaders and subject leaders. It participates in the general operation and management of one or all the courses in its subject area. Some students can be members of this committee: they are appointed by students attending the course and are defined as Student Academic Representatives. They will receive training and support in their role by the Students' Union.

Moreover, the majority of the University's Committees include representatives of the students' body: members are appointed by the President of the Students' Union. The London Met University implements an active policy to encourage students' participation in University committees. The Secretariat for Quality and Standards provides training to students taking part in the University Committee activities.

13 Relationships between the London Met and external agencies and professional bodies

The London Met aims to achieve high academic and professional standards [8]. It implements a policy of cooperative work with professional, accrediting and regulatory bodies. Anyway, in this transitional period, the relationship between university and these external institutions are not governed by precise and well defined rules. In a section of its Quality Assurance Handbook (September 2003), the London Met indicates the key elements of all external accreditation activities, in order to help subject areas to achieve suitable results and to have an overview at University level. These activities are monitored by the University through the Academic Audit Steering Group, as regards strategies and plans, and the Quality and Standard, as regards organisation.

The Academic Audit Unit plays a vital role in the visits organised by external agencies. It also assists departments in the relationship with professional bodies. Although professional bodies usually have an on-going relationship with contact people within the academic department (subject contacts), the Head of Academic Audit Unit is responsible for the official correspondence with external institutions in this field. The Academic Audit Unit maintains a record of all involvement activities with professional bodies and external agencies. These records will be periodically updated in consultation with subject contacts. All the remaining formal reports concerning quality provision, such as final validation accreditation visit reports, are kept by Academic Audit Unit.

Before the accreditation visit the staff cooperates in preparing an initial self evaluation document. In order to make sure that the right procedure is implemented and that central University practices are appropriately and suitably represented, the self evaluation document must be prepared in cooperation with the Director of Academic Administration, the Director of Quality and Standards, Student services, System and Services and all the other areas which are deemed to be appropriate. Comments from competent colleagues will be collected before submitting the document to external agencies. Compilation of information required by the external agencies is a responsibility of the subject area, although the analysis and the selection of the documents that will be submitted are supervised by the Academic Audit Unit. The Head of the Academic Audit Unit can provide advice as to the organisation of visits: the subject contact identifies the main room and the meeting room for the review visit. The agency will send the draft report following the visit to the Head of Academic Audit Unit, which is entrusted with the coordination of reports analysis and the drawing up of comments. These comments must be sent to the relevant body and must be submitted for approval to the Head of Department and, if necessary, for the final approval to the Vice-Chancellor.

In the final report external agencies can indicate some recommendations: subject contact and Head of Department will be asked to propose an action plan through the departmental Quality Committee to respond to the recommendation, within three months of the publication of the report. The final report will be analysed by the Academic Audit Steering Group, which will indicate good practice and recommendations for the whole institution, to the Quality and Standards Committee.

The Academic Audit Unit will report the accreditation of a professional body to the Quality and Standard Committee.

14 Institutional audit: spring 2005

As of May 2005, the London Met will be reviewed by the QAA's Institutional Audit [9] [11].

The QAA's Institutional Audit replaces the Subject Review and Continuation Audit and its purpose is to monitor quality assurance in universities. The QAA's Institutional Audit will consider the effectiveness of the University in ensuring academic standards and quality in its course and service provision. In particular, the main objectives of QAA are: further enhance high quality in teaching and learning; ensure that the information on course programmes is as clear as possible and available to external and internal users; make sure that public funds are effectively used.

The QAA will provide judgments on the University in this field through the audit by:

– an analysis of external advice on its internal quality procedure in compliance with the QAA's Code of Practice and the Frameworks of Higher Education Qualifications

- the accuracy in managing information data which must be preserved and published by the University
- the implementation of quality assurance procedures at subject-level (including Discipline Audit Trails during the visit)
- the analysis and management of students' experience and feedback
- a mechanism to assure the academic standards and quality of collaborative provision, such as franchising and other forms of programme related partnerships.

Judgments falls into three categories: broad confidence, limited confidence and no confidence.

The judgment of limited confidence will be given if there is one or more essential recommendation.

The QAA will also carry out a subject-level investigation into the internal quality procedures implemented in the departments. These are called *Discipline Audit Trails* and for each Institution there will be four to six trails, representing about 10% of all the full-time students of that University. In the London Met there will be six trails and the QAA will inform University about the departments or subjects selected approximately four months before the trails. The aim of these visits is to verify that the quality procedures are really in place and that departmental support is effective. Moreover, the QAA checks that students' achievements are analysed by the Institution and it compares the information published by the University and students' experience. Selected departments have to prepare their self evaluation document with the support of the Quality and Standard and must comply with the deadline set by the QAA. The visit will last one day. The department of Quality and Standard suggests that each department prepares and makes available the main documents usually required for the years 2002-2004, such as the student feedback meeting, departmental quality and standards meeting, annual monitoring, handbooks of courses, samples of assessed student work, etc.

The London Met Student's Union is invited to take part in the Institutional Audit. The Student's Union believes that all students must be aware of the Institutional Audit and considers this event as a great opportunity to report their own experience. The policy of this students' representative body is to raise audit awareness and involve students in the process. The Student's Union has been preparing for this event since September 2003, by participating in University or departmental committees and keeping constantly in touch with the Department of Quality and Standards.

During the QAA Institutional Audit, the University will have the opportunity to present its main systems for quality and standards assurance and to submit them to the external analysis of senior members of other universities who will be part of the institutional audit. The Department of Quality and Standards has been preparing for the visit. More specifically, the draft of a self- evaluation document is being prepared in cooperation with the committee and departments, to which it will be handed over before being submitting to the external audit. The aim of the London Met is to show that quality management strategy and systems are intact and involve the whole Institution. All the new procedures which are also reported in the QA Handbook 2004, comply with the QAA's Code of Practice and other important external benchmarks. It is also of vital importance that all the quality assurance strategies are consolidated before introducing a more radical approach to quality in 2006. All the staff of the London Met is invited to take part in the audit providing comments and suggesting ideas about the future development of quality and standards strategy and policies. Another goal of the London Met is to consolidate the reputation of the quality management of its two preceding universities.

15 Conclusion

The last major selected Committee inquiry in Higher Education System in UK took place about 15 years ago. Higher education has turned since then from a system based on a small elite into a system based on mass participation. As a result, an external assurance of quality and standards was needed. The presence of a national, external Quality Assurance Agency, which closely cooperates with both the central Government and single Higher Education Institutions, currently meets these needs. Of course, this is a transitional period, in which past experience has been treasured, improved and adjusted to the changes.

As regards the London Metropolitan University, high premium is placed on Quality assurance procedures, as shown by the set up of a specific Department of Academic Quality, Standards and Policy Development and by of the large number of people involved in this matter at department level as well.

Particular attention is then allocated to students' outcomes, opinions and participation in the University policy. As reported in the Strategic plan targets 2004-09 prepared by the Department of Quality and Standards, quality and standards are considered of vital importance to provide and implement academic governance strategies and systems [12].

At the beginning, the aim of the Department of Quality and Standards was to design and implement regulatory and quality assurance systems for the London Met. For the next few years staff training and development is scheduled as well as an increase in partnerships and the development of new quality procedures as of 2006.

In this perspective, the Department of Quality and Standards will contribute to the creation of a Quality Network in the University to assist staff in understanding their roles and responsibilities in terms of quality and to help departmental quality committees to achieve higher quality levels at department level. Another crucial point of the next strategic plan is to implement quality assurance procedures for collaborative provision and partnerships and to create a framework with partnership-specific terminology which is appropriate to global higher education. This will enable the University to achieve appropriate international accreditation.

References

1. http://www.qaa.ac.uk
2. A brief guide to quality assurance in UK higher education, published by Quality Assurance Agency of Higher Education, 2003, pp1-20
3. Evidence to the Inquiry into Higher Education; http://www.qaa.ac.uk/aboutqaa/evidence/evidence2.htm
4. Strategic plan 2003-05, pp 1-10; www.qaa.ac.uk/aboutqaa/strategic_plan_2003/strategic.htm
5. http://www.londonmet.ac.uk
6. London Metropolitan University, Postgraduates and Professional Courses 2004-05
7. London Metropolitan University, Academic Regulation 2003-04, pp 1-156
8. London Metropolitan University, Quality Assurance Handbook, September 2003, pp. 1-127
9. http://www.londonmet.ac.uk/services/quality&standards/
10. London Metropolitan University, Managing for Quality – a holistic model by Jill Grinstead http://www.londonmet.ac.uk/services/quality&standards/q&s.cfm
11. London Metropolitan University, Institutional Audit Newsletter, N.1, Oct 2004, pp1-4 http://www.londonmet.ac.uk/Demo_Shado/library/i76477_3.pdf
12. London Metropolitan University, Strategic Plan, October 2004 http://www.londonmet.ac.uk/Demo_Shado/library/y89266_24.doc

Interlink Project:

Evaluation and accreditation systems in Europe.

A case study: the Netherlands and Twente University

Felice Francesco Carugati, Sergio Sangiorgi[1]

University of Bologna, Italy

1 Introduction

This article presents the results of a study visit in the Netherlands, in order to collect information and better understand how the main quality-assurance related topics in higher education – evaluation and accreditation systems – are experienced in one of the most advanced European countries in this field. Our main objective is to present the information gathered through several interviews. In order to understand the local history of the evaluation and accreditation system, the political reasons that drove to the setting up of the system, its existing diffusion throughout the national academic environment and the relationships between the national level and the local sites, after an introduction about the national system, we will thoroughly analyse the case of the Twente University.

[1] Acknowledgements: Our visit was made possible by the support offered by many people; a special note of thanks goes to Mr. F. Wamelink (QANU - Quality Assurance Netherlands Universities – Education Coordinator) who helped us to organise a significant number of interesting meetings. Moreover, we would like to thank Mrs. Dr. Stiekema (VSNU – Association of Netherlands Universities), Dr. H. J. van den Berg (Dip.M - University of Twente), Dr. M. Frederiks (Netherlands Flemish Accreditation Agency), Dr. Th. de Bruin (University of Leiden) and Prof. Dr. J.F.M.J. van Hout (University of Amsterdam) for their help in providing a detailed overview of quality assurance related topics in the Netherlands.

2 History of the evaluation and accreditation system in the Netherlands

In Europe, the history of system-wide quality assurance mechanisms in higher education (HE) started in the early 80s. Around 1985 the Netherlands started to build their own national quality assurance system, promoting the autonomy of higher education institutions linked to quality assessment processes. Between 1988 and 1990 the external assessment of higher education started at a national level, coordinated by associations of universities and "Hogescholen" (professional higher education institutions). As it was often the case with many other national systems, the Dutch quality assessment system was (and in some form still is) based on self-evaluation, site visits and public reports. The general model of quality assessment (Van Vught & Westerheijden, 1993) was implemented in the Netherlands up to the Bologna process. It included four main elements: a national body, self-evaluation, external peer evaluation and a published report (Faber & Huisman,[2] 2003).

The Dutch national body VSNU (Vereniging van Nederlandse Universiteiten - Association of Netherlands Universities) was entrusted with the coordination and the implementation of procedures and methods for quality assurance in HE. Quality assessments reviews, which were coordinated at programme level and conducted by a team of people on a peer-review style, featured three main objectives: quality-evaluation, improvement, accountability. Quality assessment processes performed four different tasks: assess, advice, compare and inform. The peer evaluation processes therefore assessed the quality of programmes, thus providing advice for improvement, made a comparison between programmes and provided information (to Inspectorate of education, students, and social parties/stakeholders).

The self-evaluation process, as a system cornerstone (Faber & Huisman, 2003), emphasised the contents and the level of the programme, and it served three main purposes: it provided basic information, stimulated the internal assessment and served as a preparation for the review committee's visit. For the external peer evaluation, independent peers were chosen to make up a review committee to carry out discussions with academic and administrative staff, students and alumni. Finally a report, setting out the findings of the peer review visit, was published. The study programmes were compared, using a system of clusters of related programmes, in order

---

[2] Centre for Higher Education Policy Studies, University of Twente, The Netherlands

to show the diversity in quality and the final assessment was published in a national and international context.

In brief, all public programmes were assessed according to the subject/discipline; the Inspection Agency for HE checked the quality assessment reports and could inform the Education Secretary in case of continued inconsistent performance by institutions. The Secretary of Education could warn and eventually withdraw funding to low quality programmes. The result of the described processes, as reported by NVAO – the Netherlands-Flemish Accreditation Organisation – was a gradual shift from improvement to accountability.

After 1999, along with the Bologna Process and the implementation of the bachelor-master system, the national framework for quality assurance experienced a transition period. In the Netherlands, the quality issue was considered to be one of the main challenges within the Bologna process and the national quality-assurance system was no longer perceived as the right answer to the challenges of international validity and credibility of degrees. To meet the European objectives, it was decided to implement a system of accreditation. The accreditation process represents the culmination of a well-functioning system of quality assessment, based on the granting a quality and validation mark if a study programme meets specified basic requirements (Faber & Huisman, 2003). The accreditation system is based on the existing quality assessment system and is implemented at programme level[3].

Until recently, an externally legitimate judgment on the programme as well as a standard for basic quality was missing. In June 2002, the Dutch Parliament passed a new law on Higher Education, including the regulation of accreditation. The Netherlands Accreditation Organisation NVAO – the Dutch abbreviation for the Dutch-Flemish Accreditation Organisation – was established. The NVAO was set up by the Dutch and Flemish governments with the objective of establishing an accreditation system for all existing and new study programmes in higher education. The Dutch approach to accreditation seeks to safeguard (comparable) standards of quality for study programmes in higher education, with the objectives to create transparency in the education system; ensure independent quality assessment; enable international comparisons between degree programmes; enable foreign course providers to access the Dutch market and further enhance the quality of Dutch degree programmes.

The main tasks of the NVAO are: accreditation of programmes in higher education, on the basis of checks and inspections ensuring that the programme meets the demands of basic quality; accreditation of new pro-

---

[3] Netherlands Accreditation Organisation, 2003a, 2003b

grammes, focusing on the judgment of the basic quality; and, at the request of the institutions, the judgment of special quality-features of current programmes.

As it was the case with the previous quality assessment procedure, accreditation is composed of self-evaluations and visits by expert panels to judge the quality of the programme. The self-evaluations of accreditation, however, are not submitted directly to the NVAO itself. The NVAO is in charge of the supervision of the work of the authorised assessment agency, a 'Visiting and Assessing Institution' (VAI), who judges the self-evaluation of the study programmes. The NVAO establishes beforehand the criteria for accreditation according to predefined frameworks. VAIs' judgment should be based on these frameworks. The role of the NVAO then plays a vital role in the procedural evaluation and the validation of the conclusion (Faber & Huisman, 2003) made by VAI's. The main focus of the assessment is on process quality and on the improvement function, although there are some doubts about accreditation capability to maintain the quality improvement aspect (Westerheijden, 2003). The accreditation process puts a stronger emphasis on the results of the programme, on the achieved quality level of graduated students and, most notably, on the internal quality assurance. Thus accreditation strengthens the function of accountability, mainly serving as external justification and legitimacy, meaning that accreditation is an assurance for basic quality. This implies an important contribution to the international recognition of the higher education.

Regarding the international features of accreditation, also foreign (accreditation) organisations can be considered as VAIs in the Netherlands. Organisations may apply for the status of VAI, provided that their assessment criteria and method fit the Dutch framework.

Accreditation is a key condition for funding, student aid and recognised degrees of higher education institutions (Netherlands Accreditation Organisation, 2003a, 2003b). One of the main assumptions of the accreditation system is to start nationally and to expand the system at international (European) level.

The new accreditation system, under which courses may only be assessed for accreditation purposes by completely independent organisations, came into force in 2003. Until 2003 it was the VSNU that assessed university education and research on the basis of independent peer reviews. In 2004 the VSNU set up the **Quality Assurance Netherlands Universities** (QANU) foundation, a new organisation originated from the VSNU's Quality Department. QANU's main task is now to assess the quality of university teaching and research as a self-contained and completely independent organisation. QANU has been certified by VAI, one of the as-

sessment institutions approved by the Dutch-Flemish Accreditation Organisation (NVAO). As previously mentioned, accreditation is a prerequisite for government funding of courses, the right to award official degrees
and the allowance of student grants and loans. Furthermore, the NVAO assesses whether the length of courses can be extended: in 2003 it granted
extensions to 22 Master's courses. According to VSNU's annual report in
2003, the change-over to the new accreditation system involved more bu-
reaucracy and multi-layered assessment procedures and thus increasing the
cost of accreditation for universities.

The whole Dutch University system, and the Higher professional system
as well, is actually involved in quality assurance processes. Fourteen universities are therefore subject to accreditation processes. We would now
like to point out some data included in the VSNU annual report in 2003:

STUDENTS
  • 188,937 students enrolled at the universities
  • 80% of the students obtained a university degree

HUMAN RESOURCES
  • 51,307 university staff, 54% of them academic staff

3 Theoretical assumptions and methods

To describe the main features of the accreditation process in the Netherlands, we will refer to an official guide published by QANU[4].

According to the Dutch law (i.e. the Higher Education and Research
Act), accreditation is 'the quality mark for educational programmes'. The
authority issuing this quality mark is the NVAO.

To determine the quality of a degree programme, the VAIs (the Dutch
abbreviation is VBI and, as previously mentioned, QANU is one of its certified agencies) appoint a panel of independent experts to form an opinion
about each programme to be accredited.

The QANU assessment protocol reflects the structure of the internal
quality assurance systems operated by institutions of higher education and
degree programmes, since these institutions and programmes are responsible for the quality of the education they provide. QANU's protocol offers
an operational description of the 'basic quality', i.e. the minimum standards (intended to be at a fairly high level) to be met by an academic degree programme. It provides criteria to describe the academic orientation

---

[4] QANU Protocol - Guide to external quality assessment of bachelor's and master's degree programmes in research-oriented universities - 2004

of the programme and of the level that bachelor's and master's degree programmes in research-oriented universities are expected to attain. The protocol helps programmes to indicate how they implement educational innovations and how they keep the programme in line with changing social, professional and academic requirements. This can be done within each programme's own specific objectives and considering internal quality assurance standards.

The improvement function (facilitating improvement of the quality of the programme) and the accountability function (providing a basis for public accountability about programme quality) remain integral parts of the quality assessment. The quality mark function (judging the quality of the programme to provide a basis for accreditation) is a new addition.

The accreditation decision taken by the NVAO, does not have an immediate improvement function, it simply states whether a specific programme meets the relevant basic quality standards or not. This decision is based on the assessment of the topics and facets and on the panel's overall judgment about the programme. The quality mark function of accreditation reinforces the accountability function because the panel's judgment is validated by the NVAO. This certifies that the programme's quality justifies state funding (where applicable), the issue of degree certificates and student grants.

The institutions providing the programmes are free to draft their own improvement policy in response to an external assessment. The panel's recommendations can be of assistance in this context.

3.1 The accreditation process in brief

To summarise the accreditation process, the following steps to obtain accreditation can be pointed out:

- The University clinches an agreement with an authorised assessment agency (VAI) concerning the external assessment of the programme. The agency appoints an assessment panel.
- The programme staff carries out a self-evaluation of the programme in accordance with the agency's assessment protocol. This self-evaluation records the results of a structured internal quality assurance procedure in a report that is then sent to the agency.
- The agency decides whether the self-evaluation report is explicit and informative enough in compliance with the NVAO's assessment meeting requirements.

- The assessment panel determines the quality of the programme on the basis of the self-evaluation report and the interviews held during a site visit, and decide whether the programme meets accreditation criteria.
- The assessment panel's decision is laid down in a report submitted to the University by the agency.
- At least one year before the expiry of the current accreditation for the programme, the institution submits an application for renewal of the accreditation to the NVAO. This application is accompanied by the assessment panel's report. The assessment must describe the situation in place no more than one year before the submission of the application.
- The NVAO evaluates the report prepared by the agency and the overall decision concerning the quality of the programme laid down in that report, and checks their compliance with accreditation criteria.
- The NVAO decides whether to renew the accreditation within three months from receipt of application.
- If the NVAO's decision is favourable, then the programme accreditation is renewed for a period of six years starting from the date of expiry of the old accreditation.
- When the accreditation is withheld or not renewed, the institution loses its rights to government financing for the programme and cannot issue degrees in the relevant field. The Institution has the opportunity to improve and repair quality shortcomings and apply for a new accreditation process during a two-year period, but in the mean time student enrolment must be suspended.

An example of an assessment timetable may be the QANU's assessment schedule, in which preparations for renewal of the accreditation begin 36 months before the expiry of the current accreditation as the point of departure for national assessment of related degree programmes. This timetable is summarised in Table 1.

3.2 Assessment protocol (QANU)

The Dutch law prescribes which quality aspects must be considered during the assessment of a degree programme for the purpose of obtaining accreditation (Higher Education and Research Act [Dutch abbreviation WHW], art. 5a8).

Taking these legal provisions as its basis, the NVAO has formulated an assessment protocol that forms part of its 'Accreditation framework for existing degree courses in higher education'. In this protocol, various aspects of quality are pointed out, which are referred to by the NVAO as topics.

The NVAO assesses degree programmes on the basis of the following topics:

1. Objectives of the degree course
2. Programme
3. Deployment of staff
4. Facilities and provisions
5. Internal quality assurance
6. Results

Table 1. Nationwide assessment timetable (QUANU)[5]

Period	Activity
36 months before expiry of accreditation	QANU reminds the institutions involved of the need for assessment and asks them whether they wish to participate in the assessment process. QANU and the participating institutions make formal agreements about the performance of the assessment.
24 to 34 months before expiry of accreditation	QANU appoints the external assessment panel. The course provider conducts a self-evaluation and records the results in a self-evaluation report.
12 to 24 months before expiry of accreditation	The external assessment panel assesses the degree courses in question and reports on its findings. The panel's assessment reports are sent to the institutions concerned.
Not less than 12 months before expiry of accreditation	The institutions submit the application for renewal of accreditation, accompanied by the report of the assessment panel, to the NVAO for each degree programme involved.

These topics are further subdivided into what NVAO calls facets, which are assessed with reference to criteria, the decision-making rules on the basis of which the VAI's assessment panels come to an overall judgment as

---

[5] QANU Protocol, 2004

to whether the quality of the programme is adequate or not. This largely defines the reference framework for an assessment agency. However, as the NVAO protocol states on page 14: 'The NVAO's accreditation framework for existing degree courses only provides a broad outline and leaves room for institutes to make their own choices and for VAIs to make their own interpretations.

4 Relations between the national centre of evaluation - accreditation and local sites

As described in section 2, the initiative for accreditation rests with universities: the law requires that one year before the expiry of the current accreditation universities submit an application for renewal of the accreditation to the NVAO. In this application universities describe a number of features of the degree programme, including its level (bachelor's or master's) and orientation (higher professional education or academic education). The application must be accompanied by an assessment report prepared by an authorised inspection and assessment agency. This means that the institution will have to approach such an agency well before the current accreditation expires, and request an external assessment of the degree programme in question.

The NVAO grants accreditation to a degree programme on the basis of this external assessment. Accreditation occurs in accordance with the rules laid down in the 'Accreditation framework for existing degree courses in higher education', which consists of an assessment protocol, decision rules, criteria for judging the assessment method, the report produced by the agency and a description of the procedure to achieve accreditation. Separate accreditation is necessary for each bachelor's or master's programme, and an assessment report prepared by an authorised assessment agency must be submitted for each programme.

5 The University of Twente case study

The University of Twente is one of the smallest Dutch universities in terms of numbers of students and budget, but has a high and long-standing reputation for quality and its market share has been growing in recent years. The University of Twente represents a special case in the Netherlands: it is a very young university, since it was founded in 1961 and its purpose is clearly stated: revitalise the Twente region.

The University of Twente is the only American-style campus university in the Netherlands. Its campus integrates education, accommodation and sports facilities on a surface area of approximately 150 ha. The campus area includes over 100 buildings and 2,000 accommodation units, along with sport and cultural facilities, laboratory facilities and a catering/shopping centre to serve roughly 8,000 students.

The declared mission of the University of Twente is to be an entrepreneurial research university aiming at excellent education, research at internationally recognised level and academic entrepreneurship.

The focal points of its strategic development are:

- Institutional Profile (highly specialised in the engineering/design/problem-solving area).
- Education System (based on the Major, Minor[6], Bachelor's and Master's courses structure) represented by 5 Faculties, offering programmes in Science & Engineering, social & behavioural sciences (social sciences since the early 70s, behavioural sciences since 80s) and health-related – medical sciences (since 90s).
- Research, focused on deploying knowledge to the benefit of the local community, explicitly supporting innovation through a strong relationship with local authorities and enterprises.

In detail, the number of students (2003-2004) can be divided as follows:

- *Bachelor / master students*   7,058 students
- *PhD students*   627 (275 are international) students

The University of Twente has been recently reorganised to achieve a better balance between scientific and non-scientific staff. In 2003 scientific personnel amounted to 1,477 people (1,284 people in 1999) and 1,241 non scientific personnel (1,338 people in 1999).

The organisational and governance structures of Twente University were modified in order to better meet institutional objectives by separating education and research and to increase organisational transparency (see Fig. 1 and 2)[7].

The organisational structure shows the considerable autonomy of Faculties and Research Institutes. The governance model implemented by

---

[6] "Minor courses" are 20 ECTS Courses of the Bachelor's programme, the key purpose is to have students experience a "paradigm shift" in a different field, and learn cross-functional skills. (For 2004 / 2005, 38 "institutionalized" minors are offered at Twente University)

[7] Courtesy of Dr. Hans van den Berg, Quality Assurance and Quality Management at the University of Twente (Internal Presentation, June 2004)

Twente University focuses on the important role of professional staff to support and to provide expertise to management. As shown in table 2, to support departments shared needs, research institutes and the Executive Board, a number of service departments has been set up. In addition to and in cooperation with service departments, the Office of the Executive Board supports the decision-making processes of the board. The staff is mainly concerned with policy-making in the fields of education, research, legal matters and internationalisation. The Office of the Executive Board is made up of three workgroups (Staff, Registrar's office, Operational audit) under the Secretary's (Head of Executive Board Office) supervision.

6 History of the evaluation and accreditation system at Twente University

The Twente University, as is the case with all Dutch Universities, joined the new accreditation system in 2002, after having experienced the previous evaluation system under VSNU's coordination.

The first external review, in addition to internal self-evaluation processes, under the new system was carried out in 2003 by QANU. In this implementation stage of the new system in the Netherlands, a change-over procedure was used in which 'old' external reviews were complemented by short additional external reviews to comply with the 'new' system. Three applications for accreditation were submitted between September 2004 and May 2005 by the Dutch universities aiming at accreditation by 1 January 2008 in order to timely meet deadlines.

The accreditation process certifies that basic requirements are met at programme level. At Twente University some programmes (i.e. Public Administration Study programmes) may apply for an "advanced" accreditation. Note that Twente University is between EAPAA, the European Association for Public Administration Accreditation which was founded in 1999 by early members.

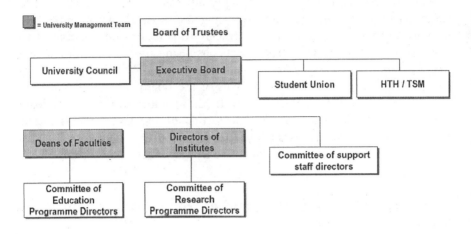

Fig. 1. Faculty and research institutes

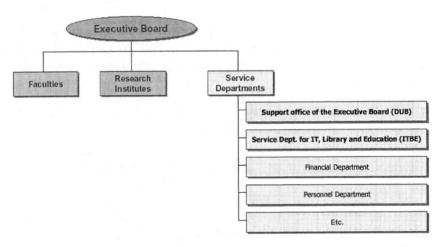

Fig. 2. Service departments

7 Organisation of the evaluation and accreditation system at Twente University

The new Dutch external quality assessment system, which was introduced in 2003, is based on external accreditation. Consequently, the internal quality assurance approach of the University of Twente is focused on the business model of an "alliance of independent faculties" which, despite the autonomous governance model, share a large number of common QA features (see Fig. 3 and 4)[8].

Internal quality assurance processes are supported and centrally facilitated by a service department for Information Technology, Library and Education (ITBE). The ITBE sub-department Education counted 19 employees in 2004 and focuses on development of expertise in instructional design, learning technologies, e-learning, quality management and services.

The quality management area is entrusted with the following activities:

- Supporting individual educations in improving their QA system and achieving accreditation
- Supporting shared initiatives to enhance QA and accreditation capability of UT
- Coordinating the Quality Management and Accreditation Platform (a Community of Practice)
- Advising the Executive Board on Quality Management and accreditation policies
- Producing recurring evaluation reports, e.g. "Scientific Education Monitor" (alumni)

At programme/faculty level[9] a QA coordinator is in charge of ensuring an appropriate management of QA processes (i.e. collecting data, networking between courses, monitoring Key Performance Indicators.) is supported by administrative staff and promotes harmonisation with Programme Director's guidelines. The following tables show the organisational model implemented for QA at Twente University. Fig. 3 presents the three different levels at which QA processes are carried out. As previously mentioned some processes refer to an institutional level (planning and control policy and procedures, business ambition and vision) within an "alliance of independent faculties". Internally each department or study programme may have either a stand-alone Quality Management System, or share common elements with other departments/study programmes. Of course, some supporting processes, such as employer relationships, may be centrally coordinated. In 2004-2005 the University of Twente developed a common internal quality assurance model system that programmes/faculties can use on a voluntary basis.

---

[8] Courtesy of Dr. Hans van den Berg, Quality Assurance and Quality Management at the University of Twente (Internal Presentation, June 2004)

[9] In some faculties, a Quality Management System – QMS – may be shared between programmes, in other faculties, programmes may have stand-alone QMS

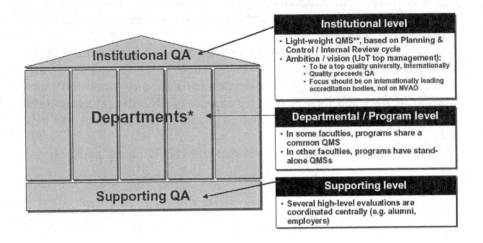

Fig. 3. Internal QA approach at Twente University

In Fig. 4 some QA characteristics and processes that may be shared by several programmes or departments are indicated. As previously pointed out, these features mainly refer to the organisation of Quality Assurance processes, whereas QA policies are generally coordinated at University level.

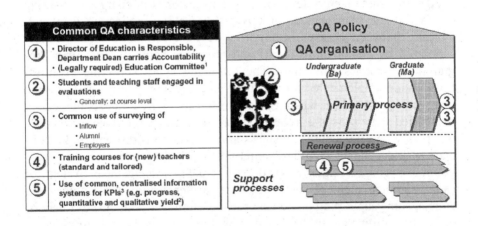

Fig. 4. Internal common QA characteristics at Twente University

8 Implementation steps and timetable of the/a process

To comply with the national accreditation system, which is based on external assessment, implementation steps and timetable at the University of Twente are the same as at all other Dutch Universities[10]. Thus, a self-report, based on programme evaluation, is produced every six years. In September 2004 a midterm evaluation review both between and within Dutch universities was under discussion. The self-evaluation process is carried out at programme level and is centrally facilitated by the ITBE department.

In addition to external accreditation, the University of Twente has introduced a system of "Major / Minor courses"[11] in the bachelor curriculum under which minors are internally "accredited".

The internal accreditation process starts with the idea of a new "minor" submitted to a "Central (institutional) Education Committee" that decides about further developments on a go/no go basis procedure. If the decision is "go" then the plan of a new minor is developed in details and submitted for advice to an internal "Validation and accreditation Committee". At this point, by means of a validation questionnaire the decision to go on rests once again with the Central Education Committee.

In case of a positive decision, the new minor course is experimented for a period of two years on a Deming-cycle procedure basis (Plan, Do, Check, Act). After the experimental period, a second internal accreditation process takes place (using questionnaires and interviews to students) and a formal report is submitted to the Central Education Committee that may decide to stop the programme or to let it go on for one further year or for five further years. When all Minor courses have been reported internally, the results will be collected and transferred for external accreditation.

This new system has been internally criticised for being somehow "bureaucratic", but it can be regarded as an interesting case of informal, autonomous organisation. As a matter of fact, it is a case in point of a formalised process within a rather informal autonomous organisation.

---

[10] Please see point 3.1 for the accreditation process in brief
[11] Please see footnote no. 6

9 Results of the evaluation/accreditation process: control and assessment

Results of all the three levels of the QA systems are monitored and assessed in accordance with NVAO criteria and a large use of surveys and KPIs monitoring is made. In addition to common QA approaches, and to facilitate and stimulate the exchange of best practices across programmes, we can highlight some local QA elements and actions:

- To promote a joint evaluation between students and teachers, discussions are organised on a six-week basis.
- Monthly teacher-lunches are a current practice to stimulate communication among teachers.
- To focus on quality assessment, an Educational Quality Commission has been appointed.
- To formalise a Deming cycle (PDCA) at teacher level, a Human Resources Management policy may be combined with educational Key Performance Indicators (for example through dedicated incentive schemes).
- To foster the inputs coming from students, an Education committee of a students' union has been appointed.
- A QA coordinator at departmental or program level dedicates time and effort to efficiency and QA improvement.

At Twente University high premium is placed on Human Resources in terms of internal courses (Didactical Introduction Courses for new teachers are compulsory in order to be appointed on a full-time contract basis) and incentive mechanisms for teaching development[12].

Internal Education processes are coordinated and driven by the ITBE department for about 4,000 training hours per year.

The table below indicates some incentive mechanisms through which the University of Twente wishes to develop teachers' professional profile. These actions refer both to the QA domain and to the specific domain of human resources management and development (job analysis and description, career plans).

---

[12] Fig. 5 is a courtesy of Dr. Hans van den Berg, Quality Assurance and Quality Management at the University of Twente (Internal Presentation, June 2004)

Incentive mechanism for teaching development			
Performance indicators	Performance appraisal	Chair plan	Job description system ("UFO")
The university is subject to a planning & control cycle	Once a year, the director or faculty dean has a performance appraisal with his direct reports	The dean draws up a chair plan in co-operation with the scientific directors involved	The universities in the Netherlands have agreed upon harmonised categorisation of job descriptions
Key part of this cycle are bi-annual meetings between executive board and heads of departments (faculty deans, scientific directors)	Appraisals cover: performance in previous period, goals for future period and conditions for performance. Prospective career development and decision on required training are included	The plan includes: the fields the chair covers based on educational programmes and research orientation of the academic staff	These job descriptions are based on a 'ladder' system. To climb this ladder, certain conditions have to be met
Support staff (DUB) prepares speaking notes for these meetings		The university has created the possibility to become full professor on the basis of non-research requirements (e.g. education)	Educational requirements are part of the conditions for academic staff
Performance indicators (research, education – information on general progress of student population) are always integral part of speaking notes			

Description of mechanism (vertical label, left margin)

Fig. 5. Incentive mechanisms for teaching staff at Twente University

One of the key challenges for quality improvement is the involvement of teaching staff in QA processes, although the time spent in QA is often perceived as an additional demand or "time subtracted" from research activities", which is the main interest declared by many teachers.

In terms of incentive schemes there seems to be a plan for actions more focused on education. According to the people we interviewed, the present scheme does not actually seem to encourage enough education improvement.

10 Costs

A rough cost-estimation for QA processes provided by the University of Twente can be broken down under:

– External costs for VAI and NVAO accreditation procedure. These costs are calculated for 15 programmes (there should be at least 35 programmes) once every 6 years and estimated costs amount to (no application for accreditation has been submitted yet) about € 150/200,000 per year for the whole university.
– An estimation of internal costs can be made assuming that every programme is attended by 6 people (a process owner, a project leader, a number of teachers and people consulted or informed about it), which

would be equal to one man/year. Under these conditions, internal costs may include both:

- running costs (self evaluation procedures, QA support at programme level, QA central support, special evaluations, in-programme routine evaluations and improvements).
- set-up/ project costs (working group, IT enhancements, programme level set-up)

Of course, the above-mentioned costs-categories take into account the present transition stage to a new accreditation system.

One issue which is often raised at a national level within the debate over the new system is the expensiveness of accreditation processes at pro-gramme level. It is particularly evident that evaluating approximately 1,280 programmes (at national level) in the bachelor-master system will be much more expensive than evaluating the previous single programmes (approximately 410 under the "old" evaluation system at national level). Moreover, high costs of accreditation are regarded by Dutch Universities as not sufficiently rewarding (according to a forecast, only five percent of Dutch study programmes may not achieve the minimum requirements for accreditation). The debate involving the University association in the Netherlands, over the evaluation level (programme, faculty or even the In-stitute as a whole) and timing (a mid-term evaluation in a six-year period is considered by Universities as a further enhancement of the evaluation im-provement function) is still underway.

11 Future steps and developments

The recently developed model for Quality Assurance and accreditation in-dicates that improvement is still needed. As it was highlighted by an inter-nal analysis of the ITBE department, the key areas for internal improve-ment include the present shift to explicit QA, as required by new accreditation system.

These are some of the areas which need to be improved:

- Transforming implicit quality assurance processes into explicit.
- Turning the Deming cycle (PDCA) into a closed cycle for all QA proc-esses.
- Working towards an integral quality management system.
- Developing and implementing student testing and assessment policy, which are still underdeveloped.

- Strengthening and demonstrating the correlation between individual courses, competence and "end terms"
- Harmonising and standardising Key Performance Indicators across programmes, thus ensuring an easy access to information through centralised information systems.

There seems to be a plan for several key initiatives at university level to improve QA at Twente.

Since people are considered as the starting point, a new people platform was implemented in 2004 to enable members to better discuss QA-related topics, share ideas and find new solutions.

At the same time, a model of a Quality Management System is under development in terms of processes. The model will comply with NVAO's criteria and it will support departments and study programmes improvement processes. Of course, tailoring initiatives will be provided to better meet special needs either at department or programme level. To this purpose, a QA manual will be made available.

To support QA and improvement processes at university level, some initiatives are scheduled also in the information-technology area. An Electronic QA system to share information, support planning and control processes all over Twente University is now under development, as well as a customised Management Information System (based on various databases), which will be gradually introduced over the next two years.

At Twente University QA improvement is perceived as a set of challenges. Some of these challenges are brought about by the many changes occurred in the past few years (the new Bachelor-master system in Europe, the new accreditation system in the Netherlands, departmental restructuring at Twente university). As previously mentioned, the implementation of a more effective connection between the organisational structure and educational Key Performance Indicators is considered as another challenge.

Moreover, a few more challenges are posed by the lack of human resources able to meet QA needs and implement improvement processes that are sometimes perceived with a limited sense of urgency.

As reported by many people, meeting these challenges requires a long-term effort and close cooperation between departments, study programmes and central support.

At the University of Twente the efforts made towards improvement and innovation are focused on both top-down and bottom-up approaches to change the mindset. Top-down approaches include organisation, finance and human resources management by considering principles implementation and adequate funding of education as best practices. At the same time, a number of bottom-up approaches towards a cultural change and involving scientific staff in educational communities are currently deployed. To this purpose, several initiatives, such as Educational courses, curriculum development, a web portal on professionalisation, an educational people network, a new QM and accreditation platform and a decentralised human resources management (in faculties) are now available.

References

1. Faber M, Huisman J (2003) Same Voyage, Different Routes? The course of the Netherlands and Denmark to a 'European model' of quality assurance, in Quality in Higher Education Vol. 9, November No. 3.
2. Van Den Berg H[13] (2004) Quality Assurance and Quality Management at the University of Twente (Internal Presentation)
3. Quality Assurance Netherlands Universities - QANU Protocol - Guide to external quality assessment of bachelor's and master's degree programmes in research-oriented universities – 2004 – www.qanu.nl
4. VSNU (Association of Netherlands Universities) - Annual report 2003 – www.vsnu.nl
5. NVAO (Netherlands – Flemish Accreditation Organisation) – Accreditation in Dutch Higher Education (Internal presentation) – Dr. Mark Frederiks 2004 – www.nvao.net

---

[13] Educational Quality Assurance Specialist – University of Twente

Creating a culture of quality: quality assurance at the University of Groningen in the Netherlands

Robert Wagenaar[1]

University of Groningen, the Netherlands

1 Introduction

In January 2003 the Sunday edition of the New York Times published a two page article headed "The New E.U." which opens as follows: 'For a college founded in 1614, the University of Groningen in the northern Netherlands is surprisingly open to change. This fall, it divided its five-year undergraduate program into separate bachelor's and master's degrees. It will soon adopt a new European credits system. And its recruiters are busy wooing young Asians and Eastern Europeans to do their postgraduate studies – in English, naturally – in this friendly medieval city.' The article focuses on the revolution that is shaking up European universities with the objective to create a united higher education system that is globally competitive.

Groningen and other Dutch universities have always been strongly influenced by foreign models and developments. In particular, the German model and later the Anglo-Saxon one shaped present Dutch higher education to a large extent. The Netherlands has a reputation for being internationally oriented. Dutch economy is very much tied up with many European countries as well as the United States. Given the international orientation of the country, it is no surprise that the Bologna Declaration of 1999 was very much welcomed by Dutch universities. The need for greater harmonisation of European higher education systems had already been felt for some time. This feeling had been stimulated by the tremendous success of international student mobility programmes, Erasmus above all, since the mid 80s. Although it copied foreign models and approaches and developed these further in the Dutch setting, the Netherlands also was a forerunner for a number of aspects. As one of the first countries in Europe, it launched

---

[1] Robert Wagenaar is Director of Undergraduate and Graduate Studies at the University of Groningen. Along with Julia Gonzalez (University of Deusto, Bilbao), he co-ordinates the projects Tuning Educational Structures in Europe and Tuning America Latina.

a national credit transfer and accumulation system, now more than twenty years ago. It was also among the first countries that set-up a national quality assurance system based on external peer reviews. Both systems were created to boost quality and to make study programmes more effective. Traditionally, Dutch higher education students took (and still take) their time to study. An average student used (and still uses) 50% more time than officially planned. Around 1980, as an effect of the oil crises in the 1970s and the level of the wages compared to other countries, the Dutch economy was in disarray. This forced the government to take action, because there was an obvious lack of tax money to pay for the growing number of students who wanted to go to university. The number of university students more than doubled between 1970 and 1992 from 123.900 to 256.731. Government shortened the official length of studies with one year and based them on credits. When this did not lead fully to the expected results, the instrument of quality assurance was introduced.

Since the launch of the Dutch quality assurance system all higher programmes have been assessed at least twice by external committees. Before this external review system was established, a heated debate took place between the higher education sector and the government. The central point in this discussion was not so much whether the Netherlands should opt for an accreditation model or a quality assurance model, but much more what kind of body should be responsible for organising the external quality assurance reviews, an independent agency installed by the government or the sector itself. A compromise was found implying that the universities themselves were made responsible for setting up their own system. However, the system itself as well as the outcomes of the review process would be monitored by the Inspectorate of Education, a separate and independent body of the Ministry of Education. It was prescribed that the main outcomes and conclusions of the external reviews should be published in a public report. For some fifteen years this system worked remarkably well, although not all reports met the same standards. For each subject area or sometimes a combination of subject areas a separate committee was established composed by independent experts in the field as well as one educationalist. These experts were mostly a group of retired professors completed with a number of active Dutch professors working abroad or foreigners acquainted with the Dutch system. Some review committees decided to compare and rank the disciplines assessed, others decided not to. If not, this was done by the public press anyway, that showed great interest in the outcomes of the external review processes.

Given the fact, that the Netherlands has a binary higher education system, in practice two bodies were made responsible for organising the external review processes: the *VSNU*, the association of universities for the research or traditional universities, and the *HBO-raad*, the association of universities of professional education for its own membership. According to the system, every subject area had to be externally reviewed in terms of required quality standards as well as comparability every five to six years. Since a binary system is not known in a number of countries, it might be useful to explain the features of the Dutch higher educational system. It is important to stress here that the Dutch secondary education system is a selective one. After primary school pupils go to different secondary schools which match their intellectual and practical level. Two types prepare for higher education: *HAVO* (Senior General Secondary Education), which covers five years of full time learning and *VWO* (University Preparatory Education including Gymnasium), which covers six years of full time of learning. *HAVO* gives direct access to universities of professional education and *VWO* gives access to research or traditional universities. *HAVO* plus one year of study at a university of professional education also allows for entrance at a research university. Universities of professional education offer undergraduate programmes which last four years of full-time study. For some subject areas one year postgraduate programmes are offered. This situation already existed before the introduction of the Bologna two-cycle system. The Dutch higher education system is well reflected in the following model prepared by Eurydice, a service of the European Commission:

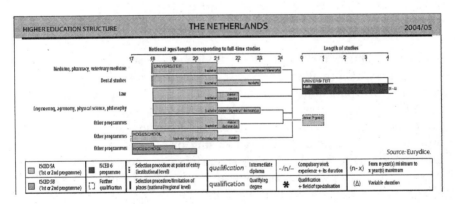

Fig. 1. Higher education structure in the Netherlands

Source: Eurydice, Focus on the Structure of Higher Education in Europe 2004/2005. National Trends in the Bologna Process (2005)

In 2002 the Dutch parliament passed two important laws on higher education. The first one re-introduced a two-cycle system and a second one introduced a quality assurance system based on the accreditation of study programmes. The term *re-introduction* is particularly suitable in this context since before the shortening of university programmes to one cycle programmes of four year, the system was based on a three-year undergraduate phase (*kandidaats*) and a postgraduate phase of at least two years (*doctoraal*). By passing the law, the Anglo-Saxon terminology was officially introduced in Dutch higher education. The use of the bachelor-master terminology did not imply, however, that another important feature of the British-American system was also expected to be introduced shortly: 'selection at the gate'. Since the 1970s *equality* had been one of the main features of higher education in the Netherlands. Until recently, the issue of selection and differentiation in higher education was experienced as a taboo. However, the discussion about a knowledge-based economy challenges the existing tradition of egalitarianism and equalizing. Initiatives are now being developed which will stimulate competition between students as well as between higher education institutions. In this setting the recently introduced system of evaluations and accreditation is taking shape. Against this background the University of Groningen has organised its present quality assurance system and is busy developing a quality culture system based on a continuous process of quality enhancement.

2 Quality assurance at Groningen University: past and present

As in other Dutch universities, the introduction of an external review system has drawn more attention to the issue of quality assurance. Since decades student evaluations are an integrated and fully accepted element of the educational process. Each faculty has its own system, but the set of questions is more or less comparable. Each questionnaire has a length of around fifteen standard questions focusing on the educational module or unit and the performance of the teacher, but also allows for more precise added questions as well as student comments. Also the member(s) of staff are asked to reflect on the unit itself and the performance of the students that have participated in it. The outcomes of evaluations are discussed in the so-called programme committees, in which students and staff are equally represented in terms of numbers. As under the law, each study programme has its own programme committee, which acts as an advisory board for the authorities who are held responsible for the delivery and the quality of a study programme. Besides the chair professors, who are officially responsible for the content of learning, this portion of the staff represents the executive board of the faculty and the director of undergraduate and/or graduate studies. The director has the day to day supervision and is accountable to the executive board.

Programme evaluation is still much less developed tool. In practice the curriculum is evaluated only during an external review process. As part of this review process a so-called 'self evaluation report' is produced, which contains information about the programme itself, the choices made, as well as statistical data concerning the number of successful students, the drop-out rate, the average duration to finish the programme and the student-staff rate. In the past the model for organising an external review was prepared by the sector itself at national level. Although a basic outline was followed, each subject area had the possibility to adjust the model to its own wishes. This is no longer the case since the introduction of a new quality assurance system. This system, which has been in place since 2004, is based on a double model. As a first step, an independent quality assurance agency prepares a report. On the basis of a positive report the higher education institution will ask for accreditation of the study programme involved. The quality assurance agency, the so-called *VBI*, bases its report and therefore its questions, on the guidelines given by the accreditation authority. This authority is called the *NVAO*, the Dutch-Flemish Accreditation Organisation. Although this organisation has been created by the Dutch and the Flemish Ministries of Education, it operates independently. The already mentioned Inspectorate of Education checks whether the organisation does its work correctly.

The previous policy that every study programme has to be assessed every five to six years has been kept in the new system. However, because of the possibility that a programme is assessed unsuccessfully and therefore cannot be accredited, the status of the whole process has been raised. In practice, the new system has proved to be much more time consuming and costly. As part of the new style external review system again a self-evaluation report has to be written for each study programme. But since the existing study programme has been split into two separate ones, the bachelor and the master, and many formal specialisations have been transferred into separate master programmes, the number of programmes to be evaluated as well as related costs have increased by 300%. At present for each external evaluation report the higher education institution has to pay a variable amount ranging from 10,000 to 12,000 euros. The Groningen Faculty of Arts, of which 19 bachelors and 26 master programmes are assessed in 2005, expects to pay around 440,000 euros to the quality assurance agency and more than 20,000 euros to the NVAO to obtain accreditation for its programmes. The size of the total amount has already led to the conclusion that this system can not be maintained in the future.

Both the government and the NVAO have announced that the system will be changed after the first round of accreditations. It is expected now that the present system of programme evaluation and accreditation will be replaced by a system of so-called 'domain (a combination of subject areas) evaluation and accreditation' or by a system of institutional evaluation and accreditation. The higher education sector as well as the NVAO opts for the last possibility because it is less costly and fits better in the present European state of affairs. The introduction of the present external quality assurance system and the shift to a domain or institutional based evaluation and accreditation system has made it extremely clear to everyone involved that the urgent need for a complete internal quality assurance and enhancement system which makes quality assurance a routine matter instead of a sort of plague returning every five to six years.

3 Quality assurance at Groningen University: future perspectives

Most faculties as well as the central university level are drafting plans to develop this so-called 'integral quality culture system' which will be a precondition for institutional evaluation and accreditation. Before this option was launched, the faculties that were recently visited by external review committees, such as Law, Economy and Business Administration as well as Arts concluded that a more structured approach regarding quality assurance procedures was required. The preparation for the visits was experienced much more as a burden than a chance to improve educational programmes, due to the reports to be prepared and the material to be collected. Because of the broadening and deepening of the procedures as a result of the new external assessment model, much more data and documents have to be gathered now than ever before. For this reason some faculties have taken the initiative to develop a plan for setting-up a special data base for quality assurance, an initiative that has been welcomed by most other faculties and by the university authorities. At present the necessary features of such a database are developed and it is expected that a decision will soon be taken to either buy an existing software system or to develop a dedicated system. The present external review system is based on 21 facets or aspects of the educational process, ranging from domain specific requirements, level, profile and study load to the outcomes of the learning process, the internal quality assurance system, the policy regarding internationalisation of education and programme maintenance. Although peer review committees have already stated that the number of facets to be assessed is far too high, in practice they play an important role in the development of a university-wide quality culture system. In the academic year 2004-2005, reports were prepared both at faculty and central level to identify the central elements of a framework for a quality culture. The different reports show many common features.

There is a general feeling that quality in the design and delivery of programmes has turned into one of the most central focal points in higher education, both nationally and internationally. This is underlined by the outcomes of the Bergen summit of ministers of education, which took place on 19 and 20 May 2005. At that conference, the *Standards and Guidelines for Quality Assurance in the European Higher Education Area*, developed by the European Association for Quality Assurance, ENQA, endorsed by the EUA, EURASHE and ESIB, were accepted by the European ministers of education. At national level government and public expectations increased accountability for the money spent. One of the ways to show accountability is a transparent quality assurance system.

Another important reason for underlining quality in higher education is mutual trust and confidence. Cooperation between teachers within a unit, school, department, faculty and university as well as between universities requires trust based on argumentation and proof in terms of the design, implementation and delivery of a study programme, as well as its outcomes in terms of attractiveness, profile, learning outcomes but also employability.

In March 2005 the executive board of the university published its protocol for internal quality assurance. It offers a model, a quality assurance cycle system, aimed at guaranteeing the quality of study programmes. This cycle contains the following steps: 1. checking or evaluating; 2. development of plans for improvement (if required); 3. implementation of improvements; 4. checking the effectiveness of improvements made. Furthermore, it identifies the main elements for quality assurance:

- study programme (curriculum) and its modules or units;
- teaching staff;
- outcomes of the learning process;
- facilities and means to organise and deliver the programme;
- internationalisation.

These elements, which have to be regularly evaluated contain the following topics:

Curriculum:

- Aims / profile of the programme and its learning outcomes
- Study programme
- Assessment and assessment policy
- Educational concept
- Evaluation of modules / units
- Placement (if included in the programme) and final project or thesis

Teaching staff:

- Didactic qualities
- Research qualities
- (Project) counselling
- Quantity (staff – student ratio)

Teaching and learning facilities

- Accommodation
- Information and Communication Technology (ICT)
- Library
- Recording system(s)
- Information system(s)
- Timetabling
- Student counselling and support
- Student reference service (for failing students)
- Quantity of supporting and technical staff

These elements or facets have to follow the already mentioned quality cycle. This implies that for these facets the following has to be established:

- Moment of evaluation and the authority responsible
- Mode of evaluation, the instruments to be applied and the persons to be interviewed
- Mode of assessment of the outcomes and the authority responsible
- Plans for improvement and the persons responsible for developing and implementation these plans
- Checking of implementation process

The protocol also requires a system of regular reporting about the internal quality assurance procedures. The university protocol is intended to be a binding guideline which can be filled in by individual faculties.

An effective implementation of the quality assurance cycle system requires that the responsible people/boards are clearly identified. The overall responsibility lies with the director of studies and/or the faculty executive board (depending on the situation). They are responsible for the functioning of the programme. They are also expected to draw-up a yearly working plan for quality assurance. In practice, an important role in the process is played by the already mentioned programme committee and by the examination board. As an option, it is suggested to install a special committee for quality assurance or to appoint a quality assurance officer. This model is represented in the following graph:

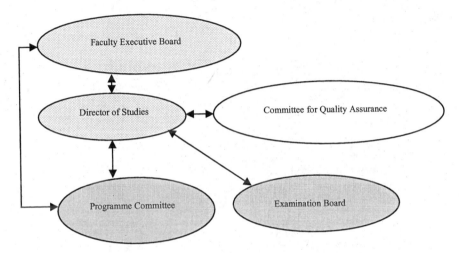

Fig. 2. Quality assurance model

The accreditation framework requires that all aspects are evaluated every six years. From 2010 it is expected that this review is no longer an external one but will be organised completely internally for all programmes. At Groningen University it is foreseen that this internal quality system will already be in operation in 2006. In the university template the following scheme is suggested to organise the evaluation process. This graph also makes a distinction between the role and level of students since they are actually important factors for the success of a programme. The facet 'students' should be seen as a subdivision of the facet 'programme':

Table 1. Groningen University Internal Quality System

Aspect	Groups / people to be interviewed	Evaluation period (minimum requirements)
Curriculum		
Aims/profile and learning outcomes (competences to be obtained by the students)	Alumni External stakeholders (professional organisations and employers) Programme committee Teaching staff External experts Educationalist(s)	Every six years; intermediate improvements every three years
Study programme	Teaching staff Educationalist(s) Programme committee External stakeholders	Every three years
Assessment and assessment policy	Teaching staff Educationalist(s) Students	Every three years
Educational concept	Teaching staff Programme committee Educationalist(s) Students	
Evaluation of units / modules	Students Teaching staff	Every three years or more often when new or unsatisfying outcomes
Placement / Final project or thesis	Students Teaching staff Examination board External stakeholders Educationalist(s)	Every three years
Students		
Entrance level	Educationalist(s) Teaching staff	Every six years
Relation secondary education – university education	Secondary and university teaching staff	Every three years
Relation university of professional education – research university education	Teaching staff universities of professional education and research universities	Every three years

Table 1. Groningen University Internal Quality System

Motivation	Teaching staff Programme committee	Every three years
Teaching staff		
Didactic qualities	Students Educationalist(s)	Every year
Research qualities	Responsible executive Researchers External experts	Research external review (every five year)
(Project) counselling	Students	Every two years
Quantity of teaching staff	Director of studies	Every year
Teaching and learning facilities		
Accommodation	Teaching staff Students Supporting staff	Every three years
ICT	Teaching staff Students Supporting staff	Every two years
Library	Teaching staff Students Supporting staff	Every three years
Recording system(s)	Teaching staff Students Supporting staff	Every two years
Information system(s)	Students Supporting staff	Every two years
Time tabling	Students, Teaching staff Supporting staff	Every year
Student counselling and support	Students, Teaching staff Student counsellors	Every three years
Student reference service	Students Student counsellors	Every two years
Quality of supporting staff	Students, Teaching staff	Every year on the basis of review interviews
Quantity of supporting staff	Students, Teaching staff, Director of studies	Every two years
Outcomes		
Meeting the anticipated learning outcomes (competences to be achieved by the students)	Teaching staff Programme committee Examination board External stakeholders	Every three years
Output (in terms of successful students)	Programme committee	Every year
Duration of studies	Programme committee	Every year

In this table the evaluation of the curriculum plays a central role as reference point for the faculty quality assurance system. The faculty, in practice its executive board and director of studies, are responsible for the transparency of process and information towards the parties involved.

4 Quality assurance and enhancement at faculty level: the example of the Faculty of Arts

As stated before, in Groningen a central role in the quality assurance process is given to the faculty level. This reflects the decentralised system for designing, implementing, organising and improving programmes. The faculty executive board has the authority to approve study programmes after having received a positive advice from the director of studies and the faculty board. The approved programme is formally confirmed in the Education and Examination Regulation. The law requires that every programme is based on such a regulation. Since all Groningen faculties have their own peculiarities, it is now worth further analysing the quality assurance process at that level. The Faculty of Arts has been chosen since it seems to have the most advanced policy and strategy not only in terms of quality assurance, but also in terms of quality enhancement. It is one of the few faculties in Groningen, but also in the Netherlands that has completely restructured all its study programmes and course units upon the introduction of the bachelor – master structure. In this process, the faculty has focused very much on the enhancement of its programmes to create a good basis for quality assurance at a later stage.

The Faculty of Arts based the shift from single four-year degree programmes to two-cycle programmes on the approach of the project Tuning Educational Structures in Europe. For the design of 19 bachelor and some 25 master programmes special committees were established with the task to develop detailed proposals. These committees received a set of guidelines to comply with. In these guidelines the concept to be applied was explained in detail. This was necessary since not only did the change to a two-cycle sytem take place, but also the shift from a semester to a trimester system, the transition from a staff-oriented to a student-centred approach and the introduction of a modularised system and a major-minor system. Detailed information was given about cycle descriptors and intermediate level descriptors to be used as one of the basic elements in the design of the programmes as well as information regarding a step-by-step approach to calculate students' workload.

As a first step the committees were asked to identify the profile of each of the programmes and to translate into learning outcomes expressed in subject specific competences (knowledge and technical skills) and generic competences to be obtained by the student. The profiles and the accompanying learning outcomes at programme level were checked by the responsible authorities before the next step could be made: the conversion of these outcomes into modules. For each of the modules it was asked to identify the competences to be trained. These had to be displayed in a grid, showing that not only were all learning outcomes covered, but also that progress was guaranteed as regards the learning outcomes to be achieved and the competences to be obtained during the programme. Before individual staff members were asked to design the course units in terms of teaching, learning and assessment approaches, the overall design of the degree programmes was assessed internally and, if required, adjusted.

The design of the course units again was based on the concept of learning outcomes and competences taking into account the number of ECTS-credits allocated to each of the modules and their accompanying student workload. The process described above took place during the period spring 2001 until the winter 2002/2003. In September 2003 all existing programmes were replaced completely by the new programmes. For current students transitional arrangements were made. In 2004 the benefit of the approach used was proved when the external review of programmes had to be prepared. It turned out to be relatively simple to prepare the self evaluation reports because most of the material and information required to answer the questions was already available. In this respect, it was also very valuable that the programme design committees had been asked to base their programmes on national and international reference points. As a follow-up of the reform as well as the external evaluation of its degree programmes, the Faculty of Arts developed its own internal quality culture system which will become operational in the autumn of 2005.

Although this faculty system is in line with the university template or protocol, it clearly has its own features. It aims at integrating the different aspects or facets that are of relevance for quality assurance, rather than the university model. The Arts model makes use of a well-known distinction:

- Education as process;
- Education as outcome:
- Organisation and facilities.

Furthermore, a clear distinction is made between the course unit or module and the study programme as a whole, as shown in the following table:

Table 2. Course units and curricula

	Course unit or module	Curriculum
Educational process	- learning outcomes of a course unit and its relationship with the learning outcomes of the curriculum - modes of instruction (types of teaching and learning activities) - methods and techniques of instruction and learning - ways of assessement - performances / counselling by the teacher - feedback on the process of learning - syllabus - course material - student load - efforts and responsibilites of the teacher	- degree profile (aims educational programme) - learning outcomes and competences to be achieved - degree/educational programme build-up and order of programme components (to achieve progression) - coherence of degree / educational programme - division of workload over the semester and academic year - feasibility of programme - teaching, learning and assessment methods - connection of secondary and higher education - international cooperation and student mobility
Educational outcome	- registration - assessment participation - percentage of succesful student	- study rate - drop-out rate - rate of switch-overs - output of 1st and 2nd cycle - employability
Organisation and facilities	- quality and quantity of teachers and support staff - timetabling of study programmes and examinations - quality of class rooms - ICT and multi-media facilities - Information and registration systems - Study programme information - Student counselling and advising - Student support	

According to the chosen educational concept, study programmes are output based. Central indicates what the student should know, understand and be able to do after a learning process. For each programme it has been tried to find the right balance between subject specific competences and generic competences. These competences are taught, learned and trained together on the basis of a domain of knowledge. Bachelor and master are clearly distinguised and are seen as entitities in itself having their own learning outcomes.

Compared to the university model the Arts model focusses much more on quality enhancement than on quality assurance. This is reflected in the the internal evaluation system organisation. The evaluation focusses in particular on the design and delivery of the study programme. Contrary to the university model, the curriculum evaluation is carried out yearly on the basis of a set of fourteen premises and questions, which covers all relevant aspects. The questionnaire that has been designed to this purpose has been included in this paper as an annex. The Dutch version of this questionnaire contains a detailed explanation as regards the questions and the available material that should be used to this purpose. The programme committees have been made responsible to produce a yearly report based on the answers to the questions, which is made available to all the people involved in the educational process. In order to carry out their work properly, the committees receive all relevant information directly or from the director of studies, such as the outcomes of course unit evaluations, course unit syllabi, information material concerning the study programme, the outcome of questionnaires to measure the rate of satisfaction among students, statistical data concerning the success rate of the programme and its units, reports concerning the connection of secundary and higher education, outcomes of questionnaires for alumni, reports concerning employability, etc.

5 Conclusion

As a result of the Bologna Process and the introduction of a new national quality assurance system, based on external evaluations and accreditation of study programmes, the University of Groningen has decided to develop its own quality culture in education. The reasons for doing so are diverse. First of all the university wants to be considered as a reliable partner by other universities inside and outside Europe. The institution plans and de-livers a growing number of joint degree programmes. It also wants to show accountability for its programmes in a transparent way. An effective sys-tem of quality assurance and enhancement guarantees that the programmes are of good quality and therefore attractive for potential students. Another, more implicit reason for setting-up a quality culture system, is to anticipate external reviews in the most effective way, whether these are based on the evaluation of the institution as a whole, a domain or individual study programmes. By investing in this quality culture now, the institution expects to limit the cost for quality assurance in the (near) future. By making quality assurance a routine process, teaching and supporting staff as well as students become fully aware of the importance of quality in the design and delivery of study programmes. This is benefit for the institution itself, but also for society as a whole.

The final responsibility for the quality of programmes rests with the faculty as an organisation. This shows that there is some tension between the desired system of institutional evaluation and accreditation and the level of formal responsibilities. In Groningen this potential tension has been avoided by the university authorities by developing a template or protocol that should serve as a model from which a faculty can deviate. The example of the Faculty of Arts shows that each faculty will set there own priorities, inspired by its internal culture and its will and possibilities to develop and enhance programmes. It proves Groningen's tradition to respect diversity within its own institution by accepting its common identity and its aims and objectives. The University of Groningen has decided to go for educational reform, as the article in the New York Times shows, because it is a tool for creating a European identity, but also for making Europe more competitive. Its newly created culture of quality is one of the major tools that will make the University even more competitive within but also outside the European Higher Education Area.

Annex

Checklist for curriculum evaluation

The following elements can be distinguished within the framework of curriculum evaluation: the educational process, the educational outcome and the means and facilities required for programme delivery.

Educational process:

- degree profile (aims educational programme)
- learning outcomes and competences to be achieved
- degree/educational programme build-up and order of programme components (to achieve progression)
- coherence of degree / educational programme
- division of workload over the semester and academic year
- feasibility of programme
- teaching, learning and assessment methods
- connection of secondary and higher education
- international cooperation and student mobility

Educational product / outcome:

- study rate, drop-outs and switch-overs (output)
- output of 1st and 2nd cycle
- employability

Required facilities and means:

- structural and technical facilities
- staff and material means
- student support: student counsellors

Educational process

1 Degree / programme profile

Premises:
The degree programme has a clearly defined profile which is based on the demands set by an academic degree on the one hand, and by the needs of society on the other hand by taking the future labour-market of graduates (of that particular programme) into consideration.
Questions:
To what extent do the available data show that the programme profile meets the demands? If necessary, which adjustments are thought to be desirable?

2 Learning outcomes and competences at programme level

Premises:
The degree programme has clearly defined learning outcomes that reflect the programme profile. Learning outcomes are described in terms of competences to be attained by the students (knowledge, understanding and skills).
Questions:
To what extent do the learning outcomes and competences to be attained by the students match the programme profile? If necessary, which adjustments are thought to be desirable?

3 Learning outcomes and competences of (individual) programme components

Premises:
For each degree programme component a total of about five learning outcomes has been formulated, which clearly contribute to achieving the learning outcomes at programme level. The learning outcomes are described in terms of competences to be attained (knowledge, understanding and skills)

Questions:
Are the learning outcomes (explicitly) mentioned in the course syllabus of each programme component (module or course unit), and explained further when required? To what extent is it clear that specific competences are practised from the descriptions? Is the level of the competences aimed for indicated?

4 Curriculum set-up and the sequence of programme components / educational modules

Premises:
The curriculum is structured in such a way that coherence is assured throughout the programme, in the different steps and components of the programme and continuous progression is made as regards the generic and subject-specific competences that have to be attained in terms of knowledge, understanding and skills.

Questions:
To what extent is it clear in practice that the programme is structured in such a way that coherence is assured and that progression is made with respect to knowledge, understanding and skills in relation to the learning outcomes and competences to be attained? If necessary, which adjustments are thought to be desirable?

5 (Division of) workload

Premises:
The programme is structured in such a way that a well-balanced division of the total workload is achieved for the programme as a whole, for and within the separate academic years and for and within both semesters. The calculated workload per programme component must correspond with the time that a typical student needs to attain the required learning outcomes.

Questions:
To what extent is it shown in practice that the total workload is divided according to the previously mentioned premises? If necessary, which adjustments are thought to be desirable?

6 Feasibility of degree programme

Premises:
The programme is set up in such a way that it is feasible for a typical student (to complete the programme within the given time frame). This implies a good mixture of teaching, learning and assessment methods, no unnecessary impediments between programme components, and sufficient supervision/tutoring by the teaching staff.
Questions:
To what extent are guarantees that a well-balanced combination of teaching and learning and assessment methods is applied, sufficient supervision by teaching staff is available, and entrance requirements for programme components are only required when a motivation as regards educational content can be given? If necessary, which adjustments are thought to be desirable?

7 Teaching, learning and assessment methods

Premises:
Several teaching, learning and assessment methods are used and have been chosen since they are particularly well-suited to achieving the formulated learning outcomes and competences.
Questions:
To what extent does the available information, in particular the educational and assessment regulations and course syllabi, assure that the formulated premises are being met? If necessary, which adjustments are thought to be desirable?

8 Connection of secondary and higher education

Premises:
The programme has been set up in order to take into consideration the entrance level of students. For first-cycle programmes it concerns the connection to secondary education and for second cycle programmes it concerns the connection to first cycle programmes (that grants entrance to the second cycle programmes).
Questions:
How effectively is it ensured that the programme is set up in such a way that a good transition is provided as regards entrance qualifications for first

and second cycle? If necessary, which adjustments are thought to be desirable?

9 International cooperation

Premises:
There is structural cooperation with foreign partner institutions. This cooperation can be joint degree programmes and/or facilitating student exchanges and recognising the academic achievements of partner institutions.
Questions:
In what way is it guaranteed that students do not fall behind schedule if they take part of their programme in a foreign partner institution, except when they are directly responsible (e.g. because they have changed their programme without consultation, or because they have not completed programme components successfully). If necessary, which adjustments are thought to be desirable?

Educational product

10 (Achieved) output of 1st or 2nd cycle

Premises:
The Faculty/School aims at achieving the following aims: successful completion of the first year of study xx% (maximum two years after starting the programme), completion of a first cycle degree based on a completed first year xx% (four years after starting the educational programme), completion of a second cycle degree xx% (two or three years after starting the educational programme).
Questions:
Does the programme achieve the set percentages? If not, why? Which suggestions are made in that case to bring about improvement?

11 Employability

Premises:
The degree programme meets a need in society if the transition to the labour market in a broad sense is effective.

Question:
Do graduates find (suitable) employment within a reasonable period of time that fits the profile and level of the degree programme?

Required facilities and means

12 Structural and technical facilities

Premises:
Sufficient structural and technical facilities and provisions are available for the delivery of the degree programme.
Question:
Are any bottlenecks in practice in the delivery of the programme as regards facilities and provisions?

13 Material and personnel means

Premises:
For the delivery of the programme sufficient quantitative and qualitative personnel means are made available in terms of teaching and supporting (administrative and technical) staff. Each programme / organisational unit has sufficient means for the delivery of the programme (guest lecturers, materials etc.)
Question:
To what extent are the assigned means actually sufficient to deliver the programme according to its original premises and set-up?

14 Student support, advising and tutoring

Premises:
A system for student support, student advising and tutoring is made available to students for the benefit of programme delivery.
Question:
In what way is the demand/need met for an adequate system of student support, advising and tutoring?

Evaluation and accreditation in Germany: the case study of the Technische Universität Berlin

Mauro Bernardini, Francesca Ruffilli[1]

University of Bologna, Italy

1 Introduction

The purpose of this paper is to present the evaluation and accreditation procedures of an important German higher education institution: the Technische Universität of Berlin. The paper starts with a general presentation of the educational system in Germany, of its evolution and distinctive features. Then, the case study of the Technische Universität of Berlin will be presented along with an overview of the implementation of national regulations on evaluation and accreditation in this institution.

The internal and external evaluation processes and the accreditation procedure will be described.

[1] Acknowledgements: We would like to thank the following people for providing us with the necessary information during our visit and for being so kind, understanding and qualified: Günter Heitmann, higher education consultant; member of the scientific staff of the T.U. Berlin, specialised in engineering curriculum design, higher education teaching and learning and teaching staff development at the TU Berlin. He is a specialist in international evaluation, accreditation standards and procedures; Dr. Stefan Jörg Arnold, Accreditation Department Manager of Zentrale Evalutations- und Akkreditierungsagentur, Hannover, ZevA; Prof. Dr. Monika Gross – Professor of the Department of Biotechnology in Technische Fachhochschule Berlin; Dr. Annette Jander, evaluation manager at the Technische Fachhochschule Berlin; Axel Köhler, graduate of TU, now part of the university staff, former representative of the students at the TU Berlin; Prof. Dr. Peter Pirsch – Professor and director of the Institute of Microelectronic Systems - TU Hannover - Chairman of ASIIN accreditation commission for Engineering - Member of European group for evaluation-accreditation criteria; Prof. Jörg Steinbach, First Vice-President TU Berlin; Dr. Patrick Thurian, Executive officer for teaching activities and study programmes (*Controller für Lehre und Studium*) in TU Berlin; Berit Zemke, office manager for teaching activities and study programmes (*Referat für Lehre und Studium*) at the TU Berlin.

Finally, some conclusions will be drawn about the present state of the evaluation and accreditation system of our case study and some suggestions will be presented as a basis for reflection for the future.

2 Overview of the higher education system regulations in Germany

Germany is a Federation (*Bund*) made of single Federal States (*Länder*) which are in charge of higher education, research and development.

German higher education institutions are autonomous, self-governing bodies and they consequently develop courses and study regulations according to their own priorities and strategies. These regulations must comply with the respective State laws and regulations and must be approved by the incumbent State Minister. Regulations are only recommendations and must not be implemented in every detail. However, they were created to guarantee common contents for higher education and thus foster accepted standards and mutual recognition in Germany, especially in the first two years of higher education, allowing students to switch from one institution to another at national level.

A specific Anti-Fraud Act protects the academic degrees awarded by German higher education institutions. Under the respective Higher Education Acts of the individual Federal States, academic degrees grant immediate access to the professions in Germany, apart from teachers, physicians and lawyers.

The general principles and foundations of the higher education system were set by the 'Federal Higher Education Framework Act' (*Hochschulrahmengesetz*). The respective State Higher Education Acts (16 acts in total) follow the example of the Federal Framework Act to create a unified system. Some State parliaments passed a single common law for the higher education system, others passed up to four (slightly different) laws for Universities, Universities of Applied Sciences, Academies of Art and Music and Colleges of Education respectively. In order to achieve the necessary harmonisation level for academic studies within the Federal Republic, 'Framework Regulations for Academic Studies and Examinations' (*Rahmenprüfungsordnungen*) were approved by the Conference of State Ministers of Education and Cultural Affairs and by the Conference of Rectors.

The Federal Higher Education Framework was amended in 1998 since it entailed some disadvantages. On the one hand, teaching activities in Germany were differently regulated from State to State; on the other hand, the creation of a Federal framework regulation was a cumbersome, time con-suming procedure which tended to produce old-fashioned results.

The resolution of the Association of Universities and other Higher Edu-cation Institutions in 1998 allowed German higher education institutions to develop degree programmes leading to Bachelor's and Master's degrees in compliance with the Bologna Process. The new three-cycle system includ-ing bachelor's, master's and doctoral degrees is supposed to replace the traditional system featuring Diplom- and Magister-Degrees. Some other degrees such as medicine, law, and teacher education and training will im-plement the new cycle system at the latest by 2010. Following an interna-tional tradition, German Bachelor's degree courses lay the foundations of academic education, provide methodological skills and professionally-oriented qualifications. The "more practice-oriented" and "research-oriented" profile types are a distinctive feature of Master's degree courses. Higher education institutions devise each Master's degree course pro-gramme.

The aim of the resolution was to increase the flexibility of higher educa-tion institutions, improve international compatibility of German university degrees, enhance students' mobility and increase the number of foreign students applying for university places in Germany.

This internationalisation of higher education and the introduction of Bachelor's and Master's degrees have actively promoted the issue of qual-ity: accreditation procedures were considered to be necessary to ensure the comparability and the quality of teaching, study programmes and degrees.

3 Implementation of the evaluation and accreditation system: the Accreditation Council

The German Evaluation and Accreditation system started its activity in 1998 with the foundation of the "Federal Council of Accreditation" (*Akkreditierungsrat*), whose objective was to manage, coordinate and or-ganise the accreditation procedures implemented by independent agencies, which were either already existing, newly founded or still had to be ap-pointed.

After a three-year starting period, the accreditation system in Germany became permanent and its final statute came into force on 1 January 2003.

The Accreditation Council is affiliated to the Conference of the Minis-ters of Education and it was set up following an agreement between the Conference of the Ministers of Education and the Conference of Rectors. Since the Accreditation Council is an independent institution, it is made up of 16 members (besides the President), who are representatives of the *Länder* (4), higher education institutions (4), professional practitioners (4 employers' and employees' organisations), students (2) and foreign experts (2).

The Accreditation Council authorises Accreditation Agencies to accredit degree course programmes. Such agencies, as well as the degree programmes accredited by them, bear the quality label - *rectius* quality certificate - of the Accreditation Council (*Siegel des Akkreditierungsrates*). For example, Master's study courses can only be accredited if they are either allocated the "practice-oriented" or the "research-oriented" profile type. The Accreditation Council draws up criteria for the allocation of profile types, and allocation is checked upon during accreditation.

Additionally, the Council coordinates and monitors the work carried out by the Accreditation Agencies and it runs a central documentation office to ensure the transparency of degree course compatibility and equivalence.

3.1 Measures for building an accreditation system

The new German accreditation system makes sure that the programmes leading to BA or MA degree courses meet certain quality standards. The system makes a distinction at Master level between a theoretical and research oriented profile and a more practice-oriented profile. The system also allows programmes to go beyond the threshold standards of the accreditation requirements, but does not provide a certification for special merits or labels.

The primary objective of the Accreditation Council is to set the principles and the minimum standards that agencies have to meet in order to be authorised to accredit courses.

To this purpose, the Accreditation Council has passed some regulations that are mandatory for agency organisations. Agencies must be independent from the State, Higher Education institutions, associations of Faculties and disciplines, professional associations and businesses. They cannot be profit-oriented and must perform accreditation activities for all types of HE institutions of the Federal States of Germany. Agencies have to be organised as legal entities and include a body authorised by the Accreditation Council that has the final say on any accreditation-relevant decision. As to the accreditation procedure itself, the Accreditation Council ensures equivalence, guarantees quality, creates transparency and also encourages and facilitates diversity. Accreditation results can be considered to be equivalent only when agencies comply with a reference framework, i.e. agreed criteria, standards and procedures. Therefore, one of the main tasks of the Accreditation Council is to develop criteria agencies should apply when accrediting degree courses. The aim of the Accreditation Council is to allow higher education institutions to organise their courses as flexibly as possible, without, however, jeopardising the comparability of future study programmes. In contrast to the fairly rigid quantitative standards and specifications contained in framework examination regulations, the Council has consequently developed relatively general criteria, which provide a flexible framework for the review of degree courses. For example, standards concerning the level and work load of new degrees courses, such as Bachelors and Masters, are only based on a few general criteria. In so doing, innovation is constantly fostered.

4 The evaluation system

The accreditation system finds its roots in the Quality Evaluation system, a system for higher education quality assurance that has been operating in Germany since the early 80s. The Quality Evaluation procedure comprises the following three steps:

- Internal evaluation. For each degree programme, the University prepares a self-report describing the structure and the contents along with the opinions of the teaching staff and students. The careful survey that is conducted produces an extremely detailed self-report.
- External evaluation. A number of appointed independent peers judge the learning outcomes and their transformation into programmes and courses on the basis of the self-report and the supplementary discussions, which took place during a visit at the University.
- Follow-up. Quality assurance through evaluation is not generally a selective procedure but a continuous process. The University consequently strives to implement the recommended measures for quality improvement and may require a subsequent evaluation after a while.

Nowadays, evaluation is still carried out in higher education institutions and it has not been completely replaced by the Accreditation Procedure. The two systems coexist: accreditation requires evaluation, but evaluation does not necessary lead to further accreditation.

5 Accreditation agencies

Accreditation Agencies are responsible for the accreditation of degree courses. As previously said, accreditation is performed by assuring quality, verifying the feasibility of study degree courses, facilitating diversity and enhancing transparency. The review process assesses whether a degree course has set and achieved its learning outcomes. The first Accreditation Agencies were set up in 1995 when they started to perform their first evaluation tasks. Nowadays, they perform both evaluation and accreditation activities. Some others are specialised in accrediting certain subject areas. These are the Agencies which are currently authorised by the Accreditation Council to provide accreditation of study programmes:

- **ZEvA (Zentrale Evaluations- und Akkreditierungsagentur)**: is a generally-oriented agency which started its activities by following higher education institutions in Lower Saxony. ZEvA started offering evaluation in 1995 and accreditation in 1998. It supports quality assurance and quality improvement for academic programmes and teaching activities. Since it was set up, it has carried out more than 150 external assessments in natural sciences, engineering, law, economics, social sciences, linguistics and cultural studies.
- **ACQUIN (Akkreditierungs- Certifizierungs- und Qualitätssicherungs-Institut)** carries out accreditation activities of Bachelor's and Master's degree courses in all fields of study.
- **AQAS (Agentur für Qualitätssicherung durch Akkreditierung von Studiengängen)** performs accreditation of Bachelor's and Master's degree courses in all fields of study.
- **FIBAA (Foundation for International Business Administration Accreditation)**: it provides accreditation of Bachelor and Master degree courses in the Business Administration field of study and related areas. The FIBAA provides Accreditation of newly designed degree courses leading up to a Diploma or Magister degree.
- **ASIIN (Akkreditierungsagentur für Studiengänge der Ingenieurwissenschaften, der Informatik, der Naturwissenschaften und der Mathematik)**. ASIIN is the only German agency specialised in accrediting degree programmes in engineering, information technology/computer science, natural sciences and mathematics. ASIIN also accredits interdisciplinary study programmes in Bachelor's and Master's degree courses.
- **AHPGS (Akkreditierungsagentur für Studiengänge im Bereich Heilpädagogik, Pflege, Gesundheit und Soziale Arbeit, Accreditation agency for study programmes in special needs education, care, health and social work)** carries out accreditation of Bachelor's and Master's

degree courses study programmes in special needs education, care, health and social work.

6 The accreditation procedure

The accreditation procedure comprises the following steps:

Firstly, the University submits an application to the Agency headquarters containing a set of essential information that the Agency requires in advance. This information includes a brief overview of the study programme contents showing the programme's core purpose.

The Agency receives and formally examines the survey. Preliminary information is viewed by the headquarters and by Technical Committees in order to decide who, within the Agency, will be in charge of the accreditation procedure and how many auditors are required. On the basis of this information, the headquarters office prepares a proposal for the accreditation procedure, including timing and costs.

Secondly, the University applying for accreditation signs the accreditation agreement and submits a self-report to the Agency in compliance with the Agency's guidelines. Following the suggestions of the Technical Committees, the Agency sets up a capable audit team under the leadership of a head auditor. Applicants are informed about the members of the audit team and, if necessary, can replace one or more of its members. After receiving the self-report, the audit team starts an intensive check of the programme's technical features. Then, it provides the Head of the programme with an assessment of the programme level and informs the staff responsible of any questions and comments prior to the visit in person.

Thirdly, the accreditation team visits and interviews the staff involved in the programme. The team can ask the University to provide any further information, which is not included in the self-report, and it therefore drafts quite an extensive assessment report. For example, the audit team checks whether the intended outcomes of the degree course programmes correspond to the contents and to the organisation of teaching and learning processes. The audit team also makes sure that students' hopes and expectations about degree programmes are met, but only at a general level. This is a major difference with respect to the evaluation procedure where, on the contrary, students' opinions about each single teacher are taken into consideration.

The outcome of the on-site visit is a final report including recommendations for the Accreditation Commission of the accrediting Agency, which has to come up with the final decision.

As previously mentioned, accreditation is compulsory for new degree programmes.

Higher education institutions offering a new programme have to submit their study concept to the Accreditation Agency. A group of experts examines the application for accreditation and discusses the new concept with teaching staff and students. Experts will then draw up an assessment report in which they express a recommendation to the Standing Accreditation Commission of the Agency, which accredits courses.

The accreditation procedure might have four different results:

1. Accreditation without reservations for the full accreditation period of 5 years.
2. Provisional accreditation valid for one year. This is a temporary accreditation which is valid only for a limited period of time and it requires that certain conditions be fulfilled by a set deadline. Should requirements not be fulfilled (the audit team and the Technical Committee determine whether the conditions have been complied with during a second, cost-free visit), the accreditation is extended for the full period of 5 years.
3. Initial refusal. In this case the institution has another opportunity to be heard by accreditation commission.
4. Final refusal. If the institution receives a final refusal, the Accreditation Council is also notified of the decision.

The result of the accreditation process enables the educational institution to receive the accreditation label, i.e. the Quality certificate of the Accreditation Council – *Siegel des Akkreditierungsrates*.

7 Evaluation and accreditation at the Technische Universität in Berlin

7.1 General information

The history of the Technische Universität in Berlin (hereafter referred to as T.U.) dates back much further than its re-establishment under this name in 1946. Its roots can be traced back to the 18th century when the Royal Technical College of Berlin was founded.

After the Second World War the Technical College was "one of the pillars supporting the technological development of the terrible war machine which enabled Nazi Germany to attack other countries" (http://www.tu-berlin.de) and many professors against the war (for example Gustav Hertz and Georg Schlesinger) were forced to leave.

The Technical College was re-opened in 1946 under the name "Technical University". The learning outcomes were also redefined: all courses included "humanistic studies", and in 1948 the chairs of history, literary studies, anthropology and social ethics were established.

Students at the T.U. Berlin can now take Interdisciplinary Studies in order to learn methods and approaches used in other disciplines and to develop new approaches to complex problems.

Since its foundation, the T.U. Berlin has shown an open approach towards new ideas and reforms. As early as in 1946 the first student parliament was elected here. The reform legislation in the 1960s and the pressures of the student movement brought about fundamental changes in the internal organisation of the university. A President replaced the Rector as head of the unified administration; he/she was elected for only two years and was responsible for academic affairs. University bodies were made responsible for academic self-administration. 21 departments replaced the 9 Faculties that had previously existed. These departments were reduced to 15 in 1993. Then, in the course of the current Reform Project, 8 Faculties with increased autonomy, along with Centres of Excellence, have replaced the departments.

The 8 Faculties of T.U. are: I- Humanities; II- Mathematics and natural Sciences; III- Process Sciences; IV- Electrical Engineering and Computer Sciences; V- Mechanical Engineering and Transport Systems; VI- Civil Engineering and Applied Geosciences, VII- Architecture-Environment-Society; VIII- Economics and Management.

With some 30,700 students, enrolled in more than 50 degree courses, T.U. Berlin is one of largest technical universities in Germany. It also has a high proportion of foreign students – around 6,200 in 2004 – coming from more than 130 different countries. T.U. Berlin cooperates with more than 200 institutions worldwide in research projects and academic exchanges.

T.U. Berlin is spread over several locations in the city, for a total area of approximately 600,000 m², 6,818 people work at the university: e.g. 347 professors, 1,732 postgraduate researchers, and 2,244 personnel working in the administration, laboratories, and central facilities. In addition, there are 1,784 student assistants and 155 trainees (September 2004).

7.2 Evaluation and accreditation at the T.U. Berlin

The T.U. Berlin started the internal evaluation of its degree programmes back in the 80s. It has gradually developed an evaluation system using local peer groups first, and it then followed the evolution of the national evaluation system and went for large agencies operating in all kinds of degree programmes. It is worth pointing out here that some accreditation agencies in Germany perform both evaluation and accreditation).

Evaluation started with internal reviews or self-evaluation reports and was extended to external peer-review in 2001. Nowadays, peers are chosen from the accreditation agency in agreement with the University. Besides these external procedures, which are often required by the respective State governments, the quality assurance or quality management structure of the T.U. Berlin encompasses a wide range of tools and facilities. For example, specifically appointed people cooperate in carrying out quality management activities: four people are involved at central level in the evaluation and accreditation procedure and three to five people without any specific training are involved at Faculty level. About 90% of the students are involved in internal evaluation.

One of the key points of internal evaluation is the students' questionnaire. This questionnaire is rather exhaustive since it is made up of more than 90 questions. Students are asked questions about their course expectations (facilities, teaching, etc), and whether they are satisfied with the course. Data on students' profiles are also gathered and they allow an accurate analysis of respondents. Questionnaires are handed out during courses. The return rate is around 30/45%; 20% of the students answer by email.

Data are gathered for each programme taking part in the evaluation procedure and they represent an important part of the internal report. Teachers also fill in questionnaires, in which they are asked questions about the quality of materials and facilities used to deliver the courses.

In the stage of peer-evaluation, each Institute (which may be considered as the basic unity of the university) chooses four peers for every programme (2 academic peers, 1 external expert, and 1 student). Peers read the reports and then, during a two-day visit, they examine the programme and the conditions of its provision. Finally, they draw up a report containing a number of constructive criticisms and recommendations for improvement. The University board then discusses the report. The board generally concentrates on single tasks in order to improve some of the course features. In some cases it is possible that the University board allocates some funds to the degree programme. In some other cases, the Institute asks the State government for financial help the make the necessary improvements. The federal government and the responsible states (Bundesländer) are interested in the development and enhancement of the quality of higher education system and are therefore willing to fund programme improvements.

In some extreme cases, the evaluation outcome for the degree pro-gramme or for the single courses is a sort of punishment and financial re-sources are decreased.

Up to now, out of 68 degree programmes 43 are involved in internal evaluation and 25 in external evaluation. The whole evaluation process (in-ternal and external evaluation) generally takes from four to eight months and it is repeated every three years.

Although the T.U. Berlin regularly performs evaluation, there are some limitations connected to this procedure. Firstly, the questionnaire return rate is rather low, and the possibility of a complete automation of the evaluation procedure is still remote. Secondly, peers are frequently chosen by the Institute and are sometimes not independent. Thirdly, the University and the Institute have a hard time finding the necessary financial resources to carry out the improvements suggested by the peer evaluation.

The T.U. Berlin completed its first Accreditation procedure in 2002. In-formation and data gathered during the evaluation procedure served as a basis for the accreditation. However, as previously noted, accreditation was carried out by the accreditation team of the Agency, which checked whether degree programmes met the minimum standards required. Four Masters' degree programmes have been accredited up to now; the cost of the accreditation procedure amounts at 12,000 euro for each programme, which explains the gradual diffusion of the procedure.

Moreover, accreditation requires a cultural change that affects several University constituencies, and, like every cultural change, it takes time.

Finally, there are some substantive questions concerning accreditation that still remain unanswered, such as: what is an "effective" Mechanical Engineering degree programme? Is it a German programme? Is it a Euro-pean programme or an international programme? These are only some of the many open questions concerning the scope and future of the accredita-tion system.

8 Conclusion

Today the T.U. Berlin has successfully adopted the spirit and implemented the accreditation system procedures. Its long tradition of internal and ex-ternal evaluation has contributed to the favourable reception of the accredi-tation culture. T.U. Berlin is fully aware of the main advantages of the ac-creditation system: a better recognition of its degree programmes along with their international acceptance; a better quality of study degree courses, the possibility to attract skilled students and more resources.

Furthermore, the development of accreditation has been confronted with some challenges. The first is the need for more information and cooperation. The T.U. Berlin needs a clear organisation chart pointing out roles and responsibilities of each person involved in the accreditation procedure.

A second challenge is the need for raising additional funds. The accreditation procedure is rather expensive. It certainly pays off in the end, but it requires a substantial financial effort in the short-term.

A third challenge is coping with the resistance at organisational level. Accreditation requires transparency and it requires the organisation to re-think its established practices and procedures. Not every member of the organisation is ready for that.

T.U. Berlin is also aware that the road to accreditation entails some risks. For example, the risk of inefficiency if too many people are involved in the procedure; the risk of a financial imbalance if too many resources are invested in accreditation; the risk of building a heavily bureaucratic structure.

Striking the right balance between accreditation costs and benefits will be crucial in the next few years.

Quality assurance in higher education: the case study of the Stockholm University School of Business

Sabrina Di Pasquale, Rino Ghelfi

University of Bologna, Italy

1 Introduction

Swedish higher education is regarded as one of finest in the world. Top marks in OECD statistics are an indication of its excellent reputation.
In Sweden there are fifty higher education institutions run by either central government or private interests. There are 36 state-run higher education institutions, of which 11 are universities.

340,000 students attend higher education undergraduate degree programmes; 83,300 of them are newly enrolled students. Active doctoral students add up to 18,900, of which 2,700 are new students. Higher education is subsidised by the state. As a result, students are not required to pay tuition fees.

Higher education institutions have obtained a growing degree of autonomy and independence over the years. Nevertheless, Swedish higher education is kept to the highest standards by a rigorous quality control system. Degrees are nationally certified. The quality of education provision is monitored and regularly evaluated by the National Agency for Higher Education.

Sweden's education policy is directed at an internationally oriented environment and the internationalisation of the student body, of the faculty and of the programmes is kept in great consideration by evaluation systems. As a result, the Stockholm University School of Business evaluation system has been chosen as a particularly significant case study.

The School of Business has been awarded the European Quality Improvement System (EQUIS), one of the leading international quality assessment systems, which is run by the European Foundation for Management Development (EFMD). In the EQUIS system the international dimension is considered as the most important approach to accreditation.

2 Higher education accreditation in Sweden

2.1 A short history

Accreditation was introduced in Sweden by a new act on higher education in 1993. The aim of this act was to grant more flexibility to the higher education institutions. Universities were given the right to hold all kinds of examinations including doctoral degree examinations. Such a decentralised system required a quality control system which could create trust and make institutions accountable for their activities. This way, accreditation procedures could be implemented in order to support and control higher education quality.

The National Agency of Higher Education (NAHE) was established in 1995 to perform higher education evaluation activities and it thus replaced the older Government Agencies.

The NAHE has been carrying out quality audits, implementing programme evaluations and accrediting institutions since 1993.

Quality audits were first performed in 1995 and two rounds have already been completed. These audits may be seen as a response to the increased responsibility which higher education institutions were allocated in order to perform quality assurance activities and implement quality development strategies. After two rounds and despite the accuracy with which quality assurance procedures were implemented in many higher education institutions, these quality audits have had only a limited impact on quality development at department level. This is the main reason why the Agency decided to suspend quality audits for a while.

In 1999 the National Agency conducted its first evaluation of major quality-related features, such as the work of the higher education institutions on gender equality, student impact and social and ethnic diversity.

In 2001 the National Agency was entrusted with the task of evaluating all undergraduate and postgraduate programmes during a six-year period.

2.2 Features

The Agency performs two different kinds of accreditation activities. The first one provides for institutional reviews in a three-year cycle. At the end of the review a final report including recommendations and criticisms is drafted.

The most widely spread accreditation process is carried out every six years and it entails a deep review of all subjects and programmes. The aim of quality reviews is to perform a control, ensure development, information and comparison.

The control is carried out by taking into consideration that institutions must reach a certain quality level. Subjects and programmes will be reviewed with respect to the general higher education objectives stated in the Higher Education Act. The development of higher education institutions should foster renewal and diversity in disciplines and programmes. High premium is placed on the availability of information about subjects and programmes. This assessment procedure ends with a "yes/no" decision by the NAHE.

The accreditation general structure includes different steps. After a self-assessment, peer reviews are performed by an external assessment group of international assessors and student representatives. The on-site visit of the assessment group enables assessors to have a look at the institution and talk directly to the university staff. After this step, feedback is provided through statements and recommendations for further development. The final steps are a public report, a decision by the University Chancellor on approval or disapproval and follow-up.

The criteria and the aspects evaluations will focus on are developed in cooperation with the Agency and higher education institutions. The NAHE suggests the features that will be evaluated in the review. Partners from the higher education institution will discuss about and confirm features and criteria.

The most important aspects for programme review are: education prerequisites, processes and results.

Education prerequisites take into consideration recruitment and student groups, teaching skills, scientific expertise and opportunities for staff development; goals, content and organisation of education; library and other information support, facilities and equipment.

The National Agency for Higher Education is participating in European cooperation schemes on higher education evaluation within the ENQA framework (European Network for Quality Assurance Agencies in Higher Education).

The Swedish evaluation system partially differs from other European countries where the role of students is less important. Both undergraduate and postgraduate programmes undergo the same evaluation process, which is carried out by one single assessing panel. The follow-up of each evaluation after three years is an integral part of the evaluation process and sanctions, such as the revocation of the entitlement to award degrees, provide a guarantee of quality.

2.3 Diffusion

About 700 programmes were evaluated from 2001 to 2003. The degree awarding powers of the institution concerned have been queried in 69 cases out of the 700 evaluated undergraduate and postgraduate programmes. These programmes had failed to reach a minimum level of academic acceptability.

During the last three years 330 assessors (125 of which, i.e. 38%, were women and 121 came from outside Sweden) have taken part in the National Agency's panels of assessors. A total of 48 postgraduate and 61 undergraduate students have participated in the panels of assessors. The National Agency was particularly satisfied with the contributions made by the students taking part in the panels.

The costs for all quality reviews are covered by the budget set by the Parliament through the NAHE. The costs for drafting the self valuation report are borne by single higher education institutions.

3 The Stockholm University School of Business

3.1 General information

The Stockholm University, which is located in the capital of Sweden, is one of the largest universities in the country with about 35,000 students and more than 2,150 graduate students.

Undergraduate education is provided alongside postgraduate degree courses and research activities at the four faculties: Law, Humanities, Social Sciences and Natural Sciences.

In 1878 the first series of public lectures on natural sciences were held in the Stockholm College, which then a state University in 1960.

In 1970 the University campus at Frescati – an area just north of the city centre – was built. Today, the main University campus stretches across a naturally and culturally inspiring landscape – in and around the world's first National City Park.

The Stockholm University School of Business moved from Frescati (the University headquarters) to the premises of the College of Veterinary Medicine on the south part of Roslagsvägen/Norrtäljevägen in 1912. The area is known as Kräftriket (i.e. the Crayfish Kingdom). The School celebrated its 40th anniversary in 2002.

The Stockholm University School of Business is one of the top Nordic Business schools and provides courses in traditional business administration-related subjects. It comprises four departments: Accounting, Finance, Management and Organisation, Marketing.

The School has more than 4,000 enrolled undergraduate and graduate students and about 150 researchers and doctoral candidates.

Five Research Institutes work in close co-operation with the private public sector in both research and training: the Institute of Local Government and Economics (IKE), the Market Academy Institute (IMA), the Personnel Economics Institute (PEI), the Sweden Asia Business Education Center (SABEC) and the Stockholm International Business Institute (SIBI).

Furthermore, an International Unit plays a primary role in this School, which has entered into a large number of joint agreements with universities throughout the world.

The School of Business has 150 staff, of which 43% are women and 57% men. There are 115 Faculty members, of whom 19 are associated professors, 16 are full professors and about 40 technical and administrative staff.

The Department Board is made up of 18 members, of which two come from the trade and industry sectors and four are students. The Dean and Deputy Dean are standing members.

There is no direct equivalence between the Swedish and the British/American systems as regards Undergraduate Programmes. Degrees in business administration last three or four years. The Swedish academic year is divided into two terms running from August to January and from January to June. Each term comprises 20 weeks of full-time study, which, if successfully completed, will give students 20 credits.

The School offers a wide range of programmes and up to around 90 courses, many of which are taught in English. All programmes are accredited by the EQUIS and the National Agency for Higher Education.

3.2 The evaluation and accreditation system

The School of Business has been acknowledged by the highly acclaimed European Quality Improvement System (EQUIS), which is run by the European Foundation for Management Development (EFMD).

The EQUIS is one of the leading international systems for quality assessment, improvement and accreditation of higher education institutions in the management and business administration field. It is a voluntary system and institutions apply for assessment. Its fundamental objective, which is strictly related to the EFMD's mission, is to raise the standard of education management worldwide. Institutions must be primarily focused on management education.

The EQUIS covers all the degree programmes offered by an institution from first-level degrees up to PhDs.

In its first seven years of its existence, the EQUIS has accredited 82 institutions in 28 countries. Institutions that are accredited by EQUIS must not only demonstrate the high general quality of their activities, but also a high degree of internationalisation. Since companies recruit worldwide, students choose to get their education outside their home countries and schools build alliances across borders and continents, there is a rapidly growing need for students to identify those institutions in foreign countries that deliver high quality education in international management.

The EQUIS does not only assess degree programmes but all the activities and sub-units of the institution, including research, e-learning units, executive education provision and community outreach.

The EQUIS tries to strike a balance between high academic quality and the professional relevance provided by close interaction with the corporate world.

The EQUIS is supported by a broad international body of academics and professionals. Deans of reputed academic institutions, HR and MD directors of major corporations, directors of national professional associations, consultants and assessment experts take part in the international peer review.

The Stockholm University School of Business started the accreditation process in 2001 and has been awarded the "conditional accreditation" for education quality, internationalisation and co-operation with the business community in July 2002.

4 The Stockholm University School of Business "Equis" accreditation

To achieve EQUIS accreditation, Institutions must be able to demonstrate that they satisfy quality criteria in three equally important topics: high international quality standards, a significant level of internationalisation and corporate integration into programmes, activities and processes.

4.1 General quality criteria

The School should be officially recognised by public authorities in its national environment and should be regarded as a major quality institution by the marketplace. The School should also have a clearly articulated mission, which is understood and shared throughout the institution and recognised as legitimate by the marketplace. The School should then be significantly present in one, and preferably more, of the following areas of educational activity: first-level degree programmes, postgraduate degree programmes (including MBA) and executive education.

The School should recruit staff, develop and manage its faculty structure in accordance with its strategic objectives, have sufficient core faculty staff to cover the major disciplines and represent a reference point for its distinctive expertise.

The School should also recruit and select high quality students in its national/international environment and should be able to demonstrate the quality of placement of its graduates and should provide effective professional student services in areas such as Admissions, International Affairs, Careers and Counselling. It should also explicitly and effectively support the personal development of its students besides the acquisition of knowledge in areas, such as managerial skills, values, ethics and leadership. There should be coherent programme design, staffing, administration and evaluation, incorporating client and student feedback and rigorous assessment processes for monitoring student progress.

The School should have a clearly defined research and publication policy encouraging faculty staff to develop distinctive areas of expertise.

4.2 The international dimension

The international dimension is considered the most important approach to accreditation. The internationalisation of students, the international experience of the Faculty and the internationalisation of programmes are the main areas in which the School must be involved.

The internationalisation of students is characterised by the recruitment of students from other countries, by the implementation of exchange programmes to ensure a two-way flow of students and by the international placement of graduates.

The international experience of the Faculty is evaluated trough the ability of faculty staff to teach in English, the involvement of visiting professors, the involvement of the Faculty in international networks, the participation in international conferences and the research and publication of an international nature.

The internationalisation of programmes is evaluated trough teaching activities focused on European and global business environments, courses jointly designed and taught with partner institutions abroad, internships and periods of study abroad as an integral part of programmes.

4.3 Connections with the corporate world

The School should have a clearly articulated policy as regards its relations with the corporate world and it should be able to demonstrate a strong customer orientation, particularly in relations with corporate clients. Whenever possible, given the statutory constraints under which the School operates, members of the corporate community should participate in its governance.

The School should manage a portfolio of contacts with the corporate world, a substantial part of which should include leading companies in their national/international environment. The School should monitor the recruiter's satisfaction with the quality of its graduates.

Programmes should incorporate structured opportunities for participants to gain direct experience of the corporate world, through internships, field work and campus visits by company representatives.

4.4 Procedures

The EQUIS is a continuous process combining strategic institutional development, ongoing quality improvement and progress towards accreditation. Accreditation may be achieved, under the most favourable circumstances, within approximately one year from application if, according to the initial Peer Review, the institution meets all the necessary criteria.

1. *Preliminary Inquiry.* The EQUIS Director and his staff will provide information about the scheme and preliminary advice to the institutions that are considering application.
2. *Formal Application.* Schools wishing to enter the scheme are invited to send a formal letter of application to the EQUIS Director and to fill in the Data Sheet by providing basic factual information about the institution.
3. *Eligibility.* Upon receipt of the complete application to enter the scheme, the institution, will go through a preliminary eligibility screening to determine whether there are major obstacles to accreditation and whether accreditation is feasible within a reasonable period of time, which is currently set at five years. This stage is also designed to make sure that institutions enter the EQUIS scheme with a full understanding of both its criteria and processes. An important part of this eligibility stage is the

initial on-site briefing visit that takes place after receipt of the application and Data Sheet.

4. *Self-Assessment.* As soon as an institution is declared eligible, it is invited to carry out an extensive Self-Assessment and to write a Self-Assessment Report (SAR) covering the quality criteria provided for in the EQUIS standards. The EQUIS staff will provide the necessary advice and assistance during the preparation of the report. This stage generally lasts from six months to one year. The Institution carries out an extensive self-evaluation and drafts a SAR in accordance with the guidelines established. The SAR is intended to be self-critical rather than promotional and analytical as well as descriptive.

Table 1. Stockholm University School of Business self assessment report: table of contents

1	Preface
2	Introduction
3	The Teaching Scope of the School of Business
4	The Development Strategy of the School
5	Faculty and Staff
6	The Student Body
7	Personal Development
8	Research

However, the information provided must provide an overview of the institution's situation and to support the work of the international review team. This self-evaluation process is designed to help the institution in gaining a clearer understanding of its strategic position by assessing its strengths and weakness, by measuring the main constraints and opportunities determined by its environment and by making sure that ambitions and resources are consistent.

5. *International Peer Review.* Once the Self-Assessment Report has been submitted, a team of Peer Reviewers will visit the institution to provide an evaluation of its compliance with the EQUIS standards and to draw up recommendations for future progress. The Peer Review is usually scheduled to take place within two months from submission of the Self-Assessment Report. The Peer Review team is made up of four members, who usually come from different countries: three of them are part of the academic community and one is a corporate representative. One member of the team will be familiar with the institutional environment of the School to be assessed. The visit lasts two and a half days during which the EQUIS Peer Reviewers meet a wide variety of people representing

the different activities and interests of the institution. At the end of the Peer Review, the Chairperson orally presents the team's preliminary assessment and recommendations for future development. The Chairperson then writes the Peer Review Report, indicating the team's final assessment of the institution with respect to the EQUIS quality criteria along with its recommendations for future development and quality improvement, including advice on what remains to be done for the institution in order to qualify for accreditation. If the Peer Review team believes that the School clearly meets all EQUIS criteria and is qualified for immediate accreditation, it will ask the School and the EQUIS Director to send the report to the Awarding Body for a decision on accreditation during its next meeting. The Chairman of the Peer Review team will then write an accompanying document stating the reasons for its support of the accreditation application. In all other cases, the Peer Review team will indicate areas in which progress is necessary and will suggest steps that need to be taken before the institution can satisfy all criteria. The expectation in these cases is that the institution will enter a period of "Guided Development" with the assistance of the EQUIS team in order to reach the level at which accreditation will be possible.

6. *Awarding Body Decision.* All institutions that have been through the Self-Assessment and Peer Review process are free to request that the Peer Review report be submitted to the Awarding Body for a final decision on accreditation. However, it is clear that only those institutions that have the explicit support of the Peer Review team will have a real prospect of a favourable outcome. The Awarding Body can choose from three possible decisions. It can grant Full Accreditation when it deems that all EQUIS standards are met. It can grant Conditional Accreditation when it believes that there are significant areas where the standards are not fully met, but that the institution generally deserves immediate accreditation. Finally, accreditation can be rejected. The Stockholm University School of Business achieved Conditional Accreditation: this is the usual decision when a School applies for its first accreditation.

7. *Guided Development.* Once an institution has gone through the Self-Assessment and Peer Review process and has received the report including recommendations for future progress towards accreditation, it may choose to enter the Guided Development stage. This service, which is provided by an EQUIS Adviser under the supervision of the EQUIS Director, is designed to help the institution define and implement an action plan to achieve accreditation within a reasonable time frame. The process is designed in a way that institutions can progress towards accreditation at a speed which is commensurate to their particular situation. Progress towards accreditation must be linked to the strategic objective of

attaining credibility in the international market place. When the desig-
nated EQUIS Adviser deems that the institution is qualified for accreditation, he/she will invite the institution to resubmit a formal application
for accreditation and to enter a second Self-Assessment and Peer Review procedure. An institution may, of course, decide to work on its
own until this stage if it thinks that it has addressed all the issues raised
in the Peer Review assessment and that it is ready to reapply for accreditation. When the institution can prove that it has addressed the issues
raised in the initial Peer Review and that sufficient progress has been
made, a renewed assessment will be made with the expectation that the
institution can be recommended to the Awarding Body for accreditation.

4.5 Process management

The Dean of the Business School is in charge of the entire process coordination. This is one of his/her main responsibilities. This is a calculated and
strategic choice. The Dean represents the driving force and his/her authority is needed to coordinate, control and encourage the people involved in
the process. His/her power is needed to take strategic decisions concerning
the organisation of the School as well. The Dean was supported by a secretary dedicated to the EQUIS programme. Everybody in the faculty and
among the staff is informed, involved and updated about the accreditation
process. High premium is placed on the students. The student's quality
board, the student's union and the Alumni Association play an important
role in the process.

A full professor is responsible for the self assessment report and for the
annual progress report.

4.6 Timetable

The Eligibility briefing session for a School should take place no later than
two months after receiving its Data Sheet by the EQUIS office. A School
which has been declared eligible is expected to notify the EQUIS office
about its intention to continue with the process within a two-month period.
If a School has not made any progress as regards the EQUIS process, Eligibility will be lost after two years and the School will need to reapply.
The process from Eligibility to an Awarding Body Decision can usually be
completed within twelve months. The Self Assessment is, of course, the
most time consuming activity. It takes several months to collect and analyse the data, especially when this process involves a large number of insti-

tution members. The drafting of the Self-Assessment report will then require at least a month.

The Self-Assessment report should be submitted to the EQUIS office six weeks before the date of the on-site visit to allow enough time for the PR Team members to read the report and to prepare the schedule for the PR Visit. If the School is aspiring to an immediate decision on accreditation, the Peer Review Visit should take place at least six weeks before the date of an upcoming Awarding Body meeting, whereby a decision on accreditation can be taken. The School will have one week time to confirm the factual accuracy of the PR Report or to return its comments on it.

Two years must go by before an institution is allowed to resubmit an application for another Self Assessment and PR Visit. If the EQUIS Committee rejects a resubmission, no further application may be resubmitted for one year, unless otherwise indicated by the EQUIS Committee.

A School must apply for re-accreditation one year before its accreditation expires. The Stockholm University School of Business accreditation process lasted about one year and a half. It started in early 2001 and it ended in July 2002.

Table 2. Stockholm University School of Business - EQUIS accreditation timeline

Time	Act
Early 2001	Application
Autumn 2001	Self assessment report
April 2002	EQUIS peer review visit
July 2003	Internal EQUIS annual progress report
July 2004	Internal EQUIS annual progress report
April 2005	EQUIS peer review visit
July 2005	Confirmation of accreditation

4.7 Costs

For initial accreditation the School must pay:

– an initial sum of 7,200 €, due 30 days after the Application Data Sheet has been approved by the EQUIS office for presentation to the EQUIS Committee for Eligibility;
– a main payment of 12,000 € due 30 days after the Self-Assessment Report is sent to the EQUIS office;
– the final payment

• In case of full accreditation: 12,000 €
• In case of conditional accreditation: 7,200 €

- In case of non-accreditation: 0 €

– For Guided Development the Registration fee is 2,400 € and the Advisory Service Fee is 1,800 € per day.

Travel, accommodation and other direct expenses connected with the international peer review are to be paid by the institution. In addition, the School bears the costs of the staff involved in the project coordination, of the secretary and of the writing of the report. In the case of the School of Business the total cost of the EQUIS process - from the application to the awarding - was estimated at around 97,000 €.

Table 3. Stockholm University School of Business - EQUIS accreditation costs

Type of cost	Amount (€)
Initial payment	7,200
Main payment	12,000
On-site visit	10,000
Final payment	7,200
Coordination (six month /w.u.)	33,000
Reports	8,000
Secretary (six month /w.u.)	20,000
Total	**97,400**

5 Conclusion

The EQUIS International accreditation has been a stimulating challenge for the Stockholm University School of Business.

The accreditation has been sought even though the School of Business is being evaluated by the National Agency for Higher Education. The NAHE evaluation, that is carried out every 5 years, is not considered by the School as a chance, but as a bureaucratic chore. It is an internal evaluation process that is seen as restrictive as regards the School's objectives.

Why

Three main reasons have led to the EQUIS accreditation:

- an international recognition and the possibility of having a benchmark in a ranking perspective;
- stimulating quality studies and researches;
- attracting funds for the foreign research.

The international recognition is certainly the most relevant reason. This is a prerequisite to stimulate exchange programmes for students, professors and researchers and to give the necessary assurances to research funders.

How

The EQUIS process involves all the university staff, students and stake-holders.

A great initial effort was necessary to launch the process and encourage staff and students. Many devices such as informative letters, meetings, letter boxes, small exhibitions, informative brochures and articles appeared on the School's magazine and on the School's web site have been used.

However, it was the management's approach which played a vital role in achieving accreditation. All the process has been managed by the School's Dean and supported by the University's Chancellor.

The process supervision and the control as regards parameters is still one of the Dean's priority tasks. The authority and the power of the project leader have certainly played a vital role in the accreditation process achievement.

Tremendously serious

The achievement of the preset objectives has undoubtedly been a challenging task. The achievement of the EQUIS accreditation has deeply changed the School's organisation and management.

The EQUIS evaluation is not simply a formal analysis of the School's processes and organisation, but it judges the content of policies concerning education, research and publications. It introduces adjustments and time-schedules, should any deviation be detected.

The Self Assessment Report is a real Business Plan which thoroughly describes the School's strategies and "the dirty linen". This is the reason why the report is not considered as "top secret", but strictly "confidential".

The School's transformation from Headquarter into University Campus, which has been carried out to meet the Institution's qualifications, may be considered as an indication of the value attached to the process.

However people involved think that if the process had not been "tremendously serious", it would not have been successful.

Tangible results

The accreditation process has brought about a significant improvement in the School's management. It has enhanced coordination among Departments, teaching methods and the capability to publish on international journals. It has also increased the collection of research funds. The improvements are generally internationalisation-related. In order to be able to compete with foreign universities and research institutes and to attract students and teachers from abroad, the achievement of high quality standards is of vital importance.

They are very proud of it

The Stockholm University School of Business is extremely gratified to have been awarded accreditation by EQUIS. The staff and the students are really proud to exhibit the world recognised symbol of high quality education in international management. Furthermore the School has achieved the international recognition thus meeting one of its own most important objectives. Its vision and its mission have been clearly defined. Through the EQUIS accreditation the School now has a plan for the future.

References

1. AA.VV. (2004) How did things turn out? A mid term on the national Agency for Higher Education's quality evaluation 2001-2003, Högskoleverket, EO Print Ab, Stockholm
2. AA.VV. (2001) From Quality Audit to Quality assessment the New Evaluation Approach for Swedish Higher Education, Högskoleverket, EO Print Ab, Stockholm
3. Hämäläinen K, Haakstad J, Kangansniemi J, Lindeberg T, Sjölund M (2001) Quality Assurance in the Nordic Higher Education – accreditation-like practice, European Network for quality Assurance in higher Education, Helsinki.
4. http://www.efmd.org
5. http://www.hsv.se
6. http://www.si.se
7. http://www.sweden.se

Quality assurance in higher education. A case study: Helsinki Technical University

Muzio Gola[1]

Torino Technical University, Italy

1 Main features of evaluation and accreditation of higher education and research in Finland

1.1 The past

In 1985, a work group of the Ministry of Education (KOTA) drew up a programmatic document regarding the development of a university assessment system. Amongst other effects, this document led to the preparation of a national database containing information about students, staff members, graduates, research and funding.

In 1986, the Council of State approved an increase in government funding conditional on the adoption of measures designed to improve management. A portion of these additional resources was earmarked for a generalised university assessment process.

Since 1990, the Finnish higher education system has been binary, i.e., based on universities and on AMK - vocational educational institutions which are upgraded to Polytechnics in the field of engineering.

[1] Acknowledgements: The author is thankful to Anna-Maija Liuhanen, Senior Adviser at the HUT (Helsinki University of Technology, TKK) for a fruitful discussion carried out at FINHEEC (Finnish Higher Education Evaluation Council), and to Vice-rector Prof. Mauri Airila and Prof. Anneli Lappalainen, Director for Academic Affairs, for a very informative visit at the HUT. Thanks are due to: Ms. Kaisa Ala, Senior Advisor, for her perfect organisation; Prof. Kari Heiskanen (Head, Dept. Materials Science and Rock Engineering); Prof. Olof Forsén, (Deputy Head, Dept. Materials Science and Rock Engineering); Mr. Timo Brander, Project Manager and Quality Coordinator. Information about the past history of Finnish Quality Assurance was taken from chapter II of the H3E- WG2 report "Quality Assessment and Quality Assurance in Engineering Education", by Muzio Gola. FINHEEC publications. All the remaining data were found on Internet websites.

Quality assessment was introduced into the system in 1990. The first evaluations (based on departmental self-evaluation and on national evaluation committees) concerned humanities, natural sciences and social sciences and were completed in 1993. One of the most visible results was the reintroduction of the two-level system (Bachelor and Master).

Moreover, the early 90s saw the introduction of Ministry-university consultations, which established agreed upon objectives and financing measures. As a result, the perception was that the university database (KOTA) and the performance consultations at least partially met the need for accountability and control and that evaluation policy could concentrate on quality improvement to a greater extent.

Evaluations and reforms were simultaneously introduced in line with the autonomy and "adjustments according to the results" ideology, whereby the Ministry of Education applied only a form of remote control through quality assessment, as opposed to the previous centrally planned and controlled educational system. This self-regulation strategy is often considered as a new name for the national management of higher education through incentives. Evaluation concerned both education and research and the latter was organised by the Academy of Finland. The third evaluation, which was carried out in 1994, concerned education and teacher training.

At the beginning of 1996, the Ministry of Education set up the Higher Education Evaluation Council. Appointed for a four-year term, the Council was made up of 12 members assisted by a permanent Secretariat which raised matters for discussion and implemented decisions.

The task of the Council and its Secretariat was to assist educational institutions and the Ministry in:

- evaluating an integral part of institutional practice.
- enhancing institutions' expertise in evaluation.
- evaluating the impact of policy solutions.

Evaluation was considered as an integral part of the institution's development. The Council considered it to be particularly important for students to take part in the internal evaluation.

In order to develop higher education evaluation, the Council:

- enhanced expertise in evaluation;
- organised training for evaluation experts;
- collected information about Finnish and foreign evaluation practices in a database;
- developed evaluation methods;
- promoted research in higher education evaluation;
- fostered international co-operation in evaluation.

The idea was that institutional performance depends on the internal quality assurance mechanism standards. The audit of quality assurance systems was a combination of self-study and peer review. The focus was on the institution's self-knowledge and self-regulation capacity, as well as its willingness and ability to assume responsibility for its quality. Methods for the evaluation of teaching activities were jointly developed by the Council, universities, polytechnics and the National Board of Education.

An internal evaluation team was responsible for the self evaluation report, which was submitted to an external committee. The external evaluation team reported to the University Board, which passed the information on to the National Higher Education Council. The results of the assessment were made available to: the University Board, the deans of the departments, and, through internal channels, to the all the faculties of the university. The criteria adopted for university evaluation were defined by the Ministry of Education and were related to quality, efficiency, effectiveness and innovation.

In consideration of the differing historical development and individual characteristics of each institution, the approaches to assessment used were not always uniform. Some universities gave priority to assessing courses or individual disciplines, while others assessed departments.

The following assessment methods were adopted:

- *Institutional evaluation:* This evaluation, which was conducted and funded by the Ministry of Education, was requested by the institutions themselves.
- *Evaluation of educational activities:* This evaluation was jointly organised by the Ministry of Education and the National Higher Education Council.

Both *institutional evaluation* and *evaluation of educational activities* were based on self-assessment and external assessment.

External assessment was always preceded by self-assessment. The external evaluation team received the self-assessment report prepared by the university structures, visited the university and interviewed staff and students. The team then drew up a final report containing suggested improvements.

The final evaluation reports have been published and were made available to all who were interested.

Most of these peculiar features have been transferred as such to the present method applied by FINHEEC.

1.2 The present

From official FINHEEC documents available on the Internet[2]:

The Finnish Higher Education Evaluation Council (FINHEEC) is an independent expert body assisting universities, polytechnics and the Ministry of Education in matters relating to evaluation.

FINHEEC is appointed by the Ministry of Education for a four year period.

The accreditation of higher education in Finland is one element of the national quality assurance system. However, enhancement and assessment of the quality of education has so far been considered as more important than accreditation in Finland.

As regards evaluation methods, FINHEEC reviews the costs and benefits of the customised evaluations versus the use of a standardised method. FINHEEC also pays attention to problems created by evaluations carried out in a foreign language and to the development of a theoretical basis for evaluation projects.

Evaluation methods are developed in cooperation with other European evaluation councils.

FINHEEC promotes evaluation research, for example, by making information available to researchers. Implemented evaluation projects also offer information which is suitable as research material. FINHEEC organises evaluation research in cases where it can acquire resources for research. In cooperation with the Academy of Finland or other funding bodies, FINHEEC may support international comparative evaluation research activities.

The following is an example of the scope and reporting system (FINHEEC 2002 Institutional Evaluation of DIAK Polytechnic – presentation of the Report).

The goals and targets of the evaluation were agreed upon in cooperation with DIAK and FINHEEC. The main issues that DIAK wished the evaluation team to investigate were: 1) cultural value and mission of the polytechnic; 2) autonomy, synergy and cooperation between units; 3) exchange of credits between DIAK units; 4) administration, decision-making and organisation models; 5) centralisation and decentralisation functions; 6) leadership and 7) quality assurance.

---

[2] http://www.enqa.net/files/workshop_material/Finland.pdf
http://www.minedu.fi/minedu/education/finheec/FINHEEC%20Action%20plan%20.pdf

FINHEEC hopes that the recommendations introduced in this report provide elements for strategic planning and development of the polytechnic. The evaluation team has now completed its work and it is now up to the polytechnic to decide how to take the best advantage of the evaluation.

The words of the evaluation team chairman, Inspector Ko, are echoed in the introduction to the report:

"The title of this report, 'With care', reflects our opinion of the implementation of our recommendations. We do hope that DIAK will have fruitful discussions, clear decisions and effective implementation of these recommendations which we believe are of DIAK's best interests".

By way of summary, the Finnish system is based on institution quality audits and not on certification or accreditation. The institutions examined are Universities and Polytechnics. A Manual for quality audits has been drawn up. The ideology behind the Finnish system is not to prescribe or to check upon the presence of a specific organisation but rather to check whether the system in place really works and to what extent.

In other words, the purpose of quality audits is to ascertain the types of mechanisms institutions implement, to know what measures are being adopted and how and the way responsibilities are allocated. The system is open in that the purpose of quality audits is to find out the mechanisms through which institutions achieve quality.

Consequently, the Finnish system emphasises the responsibilities of local management and respects autonomy. Within such context, high premium is expected to be placed on Quality Assurance at institution level.

2 Quality assurance and quality assessment at the HUT (Helsinki Technical University)

2.1 The context

The HUT was set up in 1908 and it will celebrate its hundredth anniversary in 2008. It has awarded around 35,000 master degrees and 5,000 Doctoral degrees so far. It currently welcomes around 15,000 students (Master and Doctoral students).

In 2004 it awarded 960 Master degrees and 190 Doctoral degrees. It has 230 permanent Professors (there is one type of professor only) and around 3,000 total staff (half of them are researchers).

The accreditation and evaluation system of the HUT is only partially complete.

By way of summary, "Quality" processes are in place for doctoral theses, at Department level for Laboratory measurements and at institution level for university staff recruitment.

At course level, some departments implement opinion polling for students. However, the institution does not currently demand teachers to perform any form of evaluation. Only 30% of the activities are actually being evaluated.

The majority of professors favours a better organisation of teaching activities and are sensitive to quality issues. These issues are considered at three levels:

1. general organisation of quality processes at institution level
2. compliance of contests and methods with learning outcomes
3. individual teaching quality (effectiveness of teaching/learning processes).

In 2007 the HUT is going to implement a quality assurance system which is designed to meets the requirements of the Ministry of Education.

The policy implemented by the HUT is based on the idea that university excellence is to be evaluated along with teaching and research activities.

There are currently two stakeholders whose views must be taken into account:

- the Ministry of Education[3];
- the Academy of Finland[4].

---

[3] The legislative reforms enacted in 1999 compel all Finnish universities to carry out self-evaluation and participate in external evaluations. Evaluation reports are made public and many of them are published in English. Students actively participate in all evaluations. Most evaluations consist of self-evaluation and an external evaluation with international experts. Higher education institutions are assisted in their evaluation work by the Higher Education Evaluation Council (FINHEEC).

[4] The Academy of Finland provides funding for high-quality scientific research, serves as an expert organisation in science and scientific policy and strengthens the position of science and research. The Academy of Finland has a range of different funding instruments for different purposes: it provides funding for research projects, research programmes, centres of excellence in research, researchers' training, international cooperation as well as research posts for Academy Professors and Academy Research Fellows. The Academy has four Research Councils that decide on the allocation of funding within their respective fields (http://www.aka.fi).

2.2 Competence development

Employers' viewpoint is of utmost importance for the HUT. Employers are not interested in internal processes, but rather in what students know and can do after they have completed their studies, i.e., the competences they have developed.

Learning outcomes and competences are monitored in several ways, while complying with the HUT's policy to reduce paperwork as much as possible.

Firstly, the HUT places high premium on the viewpoint of the "Union of Professional Engineers in Finland", to which roughly 90% of former students belongs. Information is gathered through meetings or presentations of this Union with single Departments.

The Union carries out studies on careers, levels of salaries, correspondence of acquired knowledge and skills with career paths. Moreover, it polls the opinions of former students on the education they received, on what should be removed from or added to the Programme.

Secondly, professors receive direct feedback from industries. Around 800 out of 1,000 final theses are actually developed in industries. This brings about meetings and discussions on the competences students should have achieved in order to effectively master a subject and it fosters relations between industry experts and professors. However, this does not seem to be bringing about a systematic reporting on the part of professors.

Thirdly, industry committees provide recommendations to Departments through representatives at institutional level. However, these recommendations are often generic and suggest providing more courses in economics and foreign languages.

Fourthly, students' opinions are collected by Departments.

Finally, the quality of doctoral theses is assessed by means of a basic control system.

The quality of teaching activities is monitored in several ways in different Departments.

The Institution as a whole has not implemented a general compulsory scheme yet. According to Professors Heiskanen and Forsén, *"the operational culture here is independent, faculty members enjoy great freedom and rely on their own doing this"*. Some Departments do not show any particular interest; others, such as the Department of Mathematical Sciences, an extremely proactive faculty, are extremely engaged and devote time and efforts to it, but they only represent 7% of the University staff.

2.3 Teaching activities and learning outcomes

A vision exclusively focused on teaching activities deals with the development of knowledge of skills, while a vision based on education examines which professional figures need to be trained.

High premium is placed on "Learning Outcomes" i.e., assessing the results and competences that students have attained.

The HUT tries to foresee and define the competences your engineers will need in the nearest future, in the next 10 years. This is a far-reaching vision entailing two parts:

1. a permanent part (basic science);

2. a variable part (module structures): disciplines which deserve more attention in the last years of the degree course and which might be changed and replaced more frequently.

In order to improve teaching activities, the HUT provides an elective course of 25 credits, which is strongly recommended to newly enrolled teachers since it is relevant for teachers' future careers. This course was first organised 6 years ago and 2 sessions are currently run every year. Course contents aim at improving teachers' performance, e.g.:

- how to run a course;
- how to become more interactive (understand main teaching values, e.g., indoctrination vs. facilitation);
- how to increase motivation.

Another technique employed for teachers' development is "peer review". Two or three colleagues agree to take each other's lessons. Afterwards they draw up a partly confidential report. The HUT has also started preparing a "teaching portfolio".

Particular attention is devoted to gathering students' opinions. Students have been evaluating courses for several years and now they even do so through the Internet. Students may receive up to one additional point for each examination if they participate in the evaluation. Attention is also devoted to the dissemination of information so that students are kept constantly informed about the procedures implemented by their University.

All these initiatives have been gradually incorporated into a structured system. The Faculty "pays for" professors' teaching activities provided that certain conditions are met:

- teachers provide lecture notes;
- students' evaluation marks are sufficient (this part is now experimental);
- teachers have a teaching portfolio.

Not much is being done to improve teachers' professional skills as regards students' assessment (i.e. examination techniques). However, some efforts are being made to this purpose. Every course entails some core-competences (basic knowledge, diligence and achievements levels) which are now being made a prerequisite for achieving higher marks.

More attention is also been devoted to teaching methods. After defining core-competences, teachers have tried to identify the most effective teaching methods. Innovative examination techniques, such as public speaking about a given topic, are currently being tested.

In order to support teaching and learning activities, a group of experts has been set up at the HUT including around 8 graduates in teaching/learning problems who provide support as regards teaching matters.

Besides the Department of Mathematical Science, which is particularly proactive, other Departments are equally active:

- Electrical and Communications Engineering;
- Chemical Engineering and Plant Design;
- Department of Computer Science and Engineering;
- Department of Forest Products Technology;
- Department of Surveying;

representing about 50% of HUT's Departments.

2.4 The internal quality assurance and improvement system

It is now worth pointing out that the HUT has 12 Deans, i.e. Department Directors and that Faculty Board members are appointed among Department staff.

The system features the following internal structure:

- the Vice Rector for Teaching chairs a specific Committee for policy-making, including the Director for Academic Affairs and the Directors (and Deans) of the Departments;
- the Director for Academic Affairs (with a specific budget of his/her own) is also Head of the Teaching Office, which is composed of 2 educators and 1 secretary cooperating with Departmental Teaching Offices. Such Offices might be made up of graduates in pedagogics, as is the case at the Department of Mathematical Science, or by technical-administrative staff, as is the case in other Departments;
- the University Teaching Office supports and guides the Teaching/Learning Development Unit by providing advice on teaching methods; teachers are supported by educators.

Tutoring services are also being provided. By way of example, the Department of Mathematical Science has recruited 5 elder students to help students with their daily problems through counselling activities. Every elder student involved is expected to allocate 10 hours per month to such counselling activity.

As regards the principles of course design and provision, it is common belief at the HUT that students should be informed about the competences and the skills they are expected to achieve besides Programmes' contents.

After establishing reference "values", an *internal peer review* must be carried out to make sure that such "values" are complied with. Of course, teachers' attitudes might vary. Some teachers believe that the responsibility of learning processes is shared by teachers and students; others think that their task is simply to teach the contents of a subject and that students should take care of themselves.

3 Conclusion: ideas and trends for quality assurance and assessment at the HUT

The interview carried out at the HUT pointed out that any quality audit process risks to be transformed into an "empty shell". This is why the HUT says to be committed to the development of its internal processes in the first place, while complying with external requirements, such as Ministry requirements.

Finland has a history of commitment to Quality Assurance behind itself before the introduction of Quality Assessment and the HUT is no exception.

The Quality Assurance system was first implemented at the HUT in 2001 and developments are still under way. A pilot scheme was implemented in May/June 2005.

Even before 2001, there had been discussions on how to organise the systems of all University units. The need for an internal quality system was raised by the staff running the Units by underlining the needs of research projects. The most developed activities actually relate to the Quality Management of Laboratories.

Only later on have the needs of teaching activities been considered, i.e. after the Ministry demanded the implementation of a specific quality system.

At the HUT the Rector initiated the process. He appointed a team and then involved professors and administrators in a work group made up of about 8-9 people.

Even if the process has been favoured from the beginning, lack of re-sources (staff and money) have compromised its implementation. As a re-sult, the system has been only partially developed.

The HUT does not have an official organisation chart pointing out roles and responsibilities of each person involved. A proposal has been put for-ward to this purpose. Most formal processes have not been implemented yet.

Two people have been appointed "Quality Coordinators" and are devel-oping the Quality System of the University.

As to the formal quality assurance of Courses, a few elements have been implemented, but no coordinated and formal process has been initiated throughout the University yet. Therefore, the following questions cannot be answered for the time being: *"How often does the process take place; how long does it take to complete it; how is the process organised; who and how assesses the process; who is the 'referee' of the process results; who is in charge of the internal and external assessment; what kinds of re-ports are needed; how many of them are required; how detailed should data be; who reads the reports; what is the use of the process results; how should non-conformities be managed?"*

One of the Quality Coordinators pointed out that the question to be an-swered is: how can a high-quality teaching system be implemented? The answer was that it is important to measure how efficient teaching activities are. The following set of questions was then put forward:

– how many students apply (compared to those admitted?)
– how many foreign students apply?
– qualifications of admitted students (in marks):
         – final secondary school examination
         – entrance examination
         – secondary school career
– average time to graduation
– average graduation mark
– number of graduates per year
– how many graduate students apply for post-graduate (doctoral) studies? (in Finland the government grants money to this purpose)
– employment rates of graduates (after a predefined period of time)
– students' satisfaction (students' questionnaires)
– employers' satisfaction (distribution of questionnaires)
– quality of teaching material (how can it be assessed?)

References

1. http://www.aka.fi
2. http://www.enqa.net/files/workshop_material/Finland.pdf
3. http://www.minedu.fi/minedu/education/finheec/FINHEEC%20Action%20plan%20.pdf

Quality assurance in higher education. A case study: the Deusto University in Bilbao

Laura Morigi, Francesca Trombetti[1]

University of Bologna, Italy

1 The higher education system in Spain: a short history

The Spanish university system dates back to the Middle Ages when the University of Salamanca was founded in 1218. The present system, however, actually derives from the 19th century liberal university, which was inspired by the centralised French model. In the last years, it has experienced its greatest growth in history, while at the same time advancing towards a self-governing and decentralised system.

The Ministry of Education, along with the Departments of Higher Education in the universities, coordinates the activities of state-run and private institutions and puts forward major education policy proposals. The Consejo de Universidades sets up guidelines for the creation of universities, centres and institutes. It can also propose measures concerning advanced postgraduate studies, identify which qualifications deserve official recognition throughout the country and the standards governing the creation of university departments. The law on university autonomy provides for administrative, academic and financial autonomy. Higher education is provided by both public and private institutions.

The Ley de Reforma Universitaria (LRU) in 1983 enabled universities to offer their own degree programmes in addition to the degree programmes officially recognised by the Ministry of Education and Culture. This law also allowed private universities to be established for the first time in Spain and gave universities greater autonomy in curriculum development and budgetary matters.

---

[1] Acknowledgments: We would like to thank Vice Rectora Julia González Ferreras for her kind and warm welcome and for having helped us in understanding the University of Deusto System. Moreover, we thank Aurelio Villa Sanchez, Vicerrector de Innovación y Calidad, for having patiently explained us the Deusto Training Model. We finally acknowledge the precious time that both Ms Julia González Ferreras and Mr Aurelio Villa Sanchez devoted to us.

The most recent reform law, the Ley Organica de Universidades (LOU) enacted in 2001, promised to significantly recognise Spain's system of higher education along the lines of the Bologna Declaration. Under the LOU, universities are now free to set their own admission requirements in lieu of the national college entrance examinations.

2 Evaluation system in Spain

The LOU states that university quality promotion and assurance at national and international levels is one of the major aims of university policies. In compliance with the LOU, the Ministry of Education and Science set up the National Agency for Quality Assurance and Accreditation (ANECA) in July 2002. ANECA is a member of the European Association for Quality Assurance in Higher Education (ENQA) and it has been represented in ENQA's steering committee since January 2003. In February 2003, the Agency has joined the International Network for Quality Assurance Agencies on Higher Education (INQAAHE) and it joined the European Consortium for Accreditation (ECA) in November 2003. A coordination committee was set up in 2003 to ensure transparency and cooperation between the national and regional agencies – eight in total – throughout Spain.

The main purpose of ANECA is to certify, accredit and measure the performance of higher education provision as a public service. The Agency also seeks to reinforce transparency and comparability in order to promote quality and quality assurance in universities and, by the same token, their integration into the European Higher Education Area. It also seeks to establish accountability criteria. The LOU provides that once the introduction of a study plan is complete, universities must submit the actual performance of that study plan to assessment by ANECA. The procedure and the criteria for suspension or revocation of recognition of a degree will be established by the Government. ANECA carries out its tasks by implementing six main programmes:

1. The **Accreditation Programme:** The Accreditation Programme represents ANECA's main function and, under Universities Law, is the only accrediting body in this field. Through this programme ANECA checks compliance with given criteria and established standards, while ensuring that training results are adequate and that the skills acquired by students meet the demands of the labour market and society as a whole. The programme applies for courses of study leading to official degrees, degree courses leading to doctoral degrees and institutions offering study programmes in foreign education systems. The ANECA Seal of Quality or

Excellence is awarded to all official degree courses that attain the defined standards. To validate this process, ANECA has established a National Accreditation Committee (Comité Nacional de Acreditation) whose members have a national and international reputation in the fields of teaching and academic research, as well as in the business and professional sectors. The main task of the committee is to validate the accreditation process.

2. The **Institutional Assessment Programme** assesses university courses leading to official degrees valid throughout the national territory in order to steer improvement plans. The criteria and indicators used in this process are the same as for degree accreditation. The Institutional Assessment is developed in three consistent phases.

3. During the first one - i.e. the **Self assessment** phase - the assessed unit describes and appraises its own situation with respect to the established criteria. The result of the analysis is recorded in an Internal Assessment Report and its accuracy is checked upon by an external committee of assessors appointed by ANECA during the second phase, which is called **External assessment**. The committee then makes its own recommendations and puts forward proposals for improvement, which are stated in an External Assessment Report.

4. The Institutional Assessment Programme is completed once the **Final report** (third phase) is issued by ANECA on the basis of the self Assessment Report, which is drawn up by ANECA in light of the reports on degrees, and the External Assessment Report, which is proposed by the University as a synthesis of the recommendations stated in the self Assessment and External Assessment Reports. The University is in charge of inviting the ANECA commission to perform the peer review. Should the external assessment not be successful, the Rector will ask the representatives of the faculty that did not pass the assessment to draft an improvement plan to be assessed by ANECA.

5. The **Teaching Staff Assessment Programme**: The objective of this programme is to implement all the competences relating to teaching staff assessment. These competences cover both teaching staff contracts at public and private universities throughout the national territory, and aspects of eligibility processes. To that end, Assessment Committees have been set up and entrusted with the task of curricula assessment. The ANECA is also responsible for assessing merits in connection with the allocation of pay supplements to teaching staff.

6. The **Certification Programme** is an external assessment process to check compliance with a set of previously established specifications. Its main purpose is to inspect quality and introduce a methodology for

promoting the continuous improvement of university programmes and services.

7. The **European Convergence Programme** aims at the promoting of actions facilitating the integration of Spanish higher education within the European Higher Education Area. To this purpose,

- it fosters the dissemination of and raises awareness about the Bologna Declaration contents;
- it carries out pilot experiments in order to design and introduce degrees compliant with the Bologna Declaration and
- it supports coordinated inter-university projects for the establishment of the European Credit System.

The Internal Evaluation System of Universities is in line with each university's evaluation plans and with the II Plan for University Quality (II Plan de la Calidad de la Universidades), whose objectives are being developed and promoted by ANECA.

3 A case study: the University of Deusto

3.1 A brief history

The University of Deusto (UD) is one of the most distinguished and prestigious academic private institutions in Spain, with campuses both in Bilbao and San Sebastián. It was established in 1886 thanks to the desire of the Basque country to have its own university and the wish of the Society of Jesus to move its school of Higher Studies from La Guardia to a more central location. The Business College of the University, which was founded in 1916, was the first college and the only one of its kind for nearly 50 years in Spain. In 1973, it became the Faculty of Economics and Business Administration. During the Spanish Civil War, the UD became a military base, and after the fall of Bilbao in 1937, it was turned into a hospital and concentration camp. University life finally resumed in October 1940.

3.2 The University of Deusto today

The UD has undergone many changes since its foundation. The number of students has grown from 5,000 in 1962 to over 16,000 nowadays; the number of lecturers has risen to more than 600; eight more faculties have been set up and a large number of institutes, university schools and other kinds of centres, as well as many postgraduate degrees, such as master's degrees and diploma courses, have been created. The central headquarters of the UD is located on the opposite side of the estuary, facing the Guggenheim Museum. In 2002 the campus of the UD in Bilbao has been declared Historical Monument.

The international approach of the UD is demonstrated by a clear commitment to Europe and Latin America, having signed agreements with 211 universities in 1998 as part of the Institutional Contract for 2000-2001. With a mobility of approximately 1,300 students and 50 professors, the faculties, institutes and schools are also involved in intensive programmes, European modules and joint curricular designs at various levels while they participate in cross-border activities, integrated languages, ODL and Leonardo programmes. The entire University adopted the ECTS system in the year 1994 and currently promotes and improves its quality. Since May 2001 the UD and the University of Groningen in the Netherlands have been jointly coordinating the project Tuning Educational Structures in Europe financed by the European Commission.

The University of Deusto also participates in several ALFA (América Latina - Formación Académica) projects and was granted a UNESCO chair for the training of human resources for Latin America in the 90s. It co-ordinates the Crisis and Humanitarian Action Programme, in which 140 students, 25 experts, and 15 to 20 professors from six European universities participate, and other initiatives such as the European Migration Modules, Cultural and Territorial Identity in Europe and Christianity and European Collective Memory.

As to the governance, the UD is run by three boards:

1. **Consejo de Gobierno.** Its members are external people representing political and economic institutions in the city. It is mainly entrusted with strategic planning;
2. **Consejo de Direcciòn**. It is the executive body and is made up of the Rector, six Vice rectors – entrusted with Ordinacion Academica y Profesorado, Reaserch, Innovation and Quality, students and Language Policy, the San Sebastian campus and International Relations – and the General Secretary;
3. **Consejo Accademico**. It is the political body and its members are the Rector, the Vice rectors, the Faculties' Deans and the representatives of the Institutes.

3.3 UD's mission

Despite all changes the UD has undergone, it has always remained faithful to its original principles such as peace, solidarity and justice, which are strongly shared by the Governing boards and the staff. These principles are at the heart of UD mission.

The dedication, commitment and quality of the teaching staff are the primary resource to promote the development of the UD mission. Among the main features of the teaching staff, the following characteristics stand out:

- the professional quality of their teaching staff who is concerned with the development of students as individuals and their crucial problems, in addition to their academic learning;
- their high level of scientific authority and research competence in their chosen field;
- their interdisciplinary nature;
- their willingness to discuss and to create close relationships with students;
- their participation in networks and in collaboration with other professionals from institutions worldwide;
- their commitment to continuing education and training.

3.4 The Strategic plan 2004-2007

The reasons that lead the UD to adopt a Strategic Plan date back to the last decade. At that time a widespread need to change the internal system was strongly felt among the Governing boards and the staff at the University. When the Declaration of Bologna was signed in June 1999 and the so-called Bologna process began, the Deusto University was ready to implement the irreversible harmonisation process of the various European systems of higher education, with the aim to establish a European Higher Education Area by 2010.

The University of Deusto already stood out for its openness to innovation and development in 1994 when the entire University adopted the ECTS system. As a matter of fact, the Universidad de Deusto was the first European university to extend the implementation of the ECTS to all its faculties. During the past few years, the University Governing Board and Management have been reviewing the Strategic Plan that led to the revamping of the UD, by considering which factors and options have had a positive impact and by correcting any mistakes. In spite of such mistakes, all the university community members believe that there is a need for a strategic plan that guides the institution and its activities in order to meet common objectives. The strategic plan basically suggests that individuals (both students and staff) are the pivot element of the process and that their dedication to the task requires an appreciation of the value of individuals themselves which must be constantly fostered. The Strategic Plan is aimed at a further development of the students' learning processes independently from the Teaching Framework already in place. It entails a comprehensive development of students at personal, socio-ethical, academic-intellectual, professional and spiritual level.

The Strategic Plan, which is shown in Figure 1, is made up of 5 major strategic action lines such as Teaching Innovation, Quality Management, Research Development and Reinforcement, Promotion of Life-Long Learning and Strengthening of the University-Society Relationship. Each one of these actions entails various sub-projects featuring both general and specific objectives, the tasks to be carried out, a time schedule for the next four years, the indicators laid down to check that the Strategic Plan is complied with and the people responsible for its correct implementation.

The projects are approved at first by the Consejo de Gobierno, then by the Consejo Accademico and again by the Consejo de Gobierno. All these governing bodies meet every 3 months. The Direcciòn de la Universidad and the vice rectors are responsible for the actual fulfilment of approved projects.

The following strategic action lines describe the main processes of university activity in a selective and focused way.

First action line – Teaching Innovation

– This action line focuses on the application of common guidelines for teaching and learning activities concerning all degrees; on the customised monitoring of students' performance by means of a reinforced tutor system; on the promotion of the values associated with social justice and solidarity; on multilingualism with particular reference to encouraging proficiency in the Basque language and its significant use in the UD, as well as the promotion of capabilities in modern foreign languages and the mobility of students and lecturers within international exchange programmes.

Second action line - Quality Management

– This line is aimed at promoting an institutional culture that helps implementing common teaching and learning practices, by introducing a quality process management system in all the UD centres and services. This action line also includes the key-project on staff development, which provides for the training, assessment, motivation, promotion and remuneration of teaching staff.

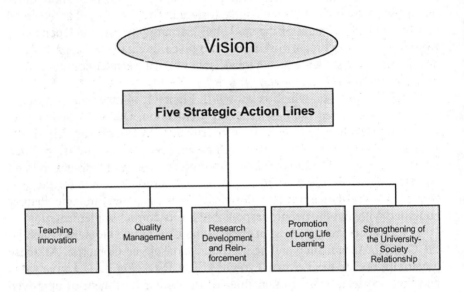

Deusto Training Model

Fig. 1. Strategic plan

Third action line - Research Development and Reinforcement

– This line promotes the Development of the UD general research activities, with particular reference to the major interdisciplinary projects of each centre and research teams, and their incorporation into relevant national and international networks of excellence.

Fourth action line - Promotion of Life-Long Learning

– This line focuses on continuous education and training and postgraduate courses, which actively contribute to the training of professionals by means of specialised programmes, both at university level and through "on line" courses. As a result, a dedicated Institute has been created in order to coordinate and promote these activities.

Fifth action line - Strengthening of the University-Society Relationship

- This action line is designed to intensify university-society relations at both national and international level with a view to future developments. This option includes projects aimed at:

  - promoting communication and cooperation with social institutions and the business world;
  - strengthening existing student associations;
  - promoting activities focused on issues of social concern such as peace and encouraging justice and human rights as well as intercultural exchange.

3.5 The Deusto Training Model (MDF)

The MDF summarises the psycho-pedagogical aspects and provides guidelines to develop teaching and learning processes by incorporating the so-called 'competence approach' into the European Credit Transfer System (ECTS). The main goal of this model is to develop a significantly autonomous learning process as well as to provide students with a comprehensive education at personal, social, ethical, academic and professional level. The MDF's objective is to achieve the highest level of development of students' capacities and to provide them with constant support in their academic progress. Students will thus acquire a method enabling them to continue learning by themselves, linking their academic development to continual training throughout their work and professional life.

The MDF bear the shape of a pyramid as shown in Figure 2.

The four sides at the pyramid's base represent the fundamental principles of the UD's mission: The UD is an organisation that is ethically and socially committed, works in teams, leads and encourages staff and places high premium on students. Each side represents the essential elements for the development of the teaching and learning process:

1. instrumental, interpersonal and systematic **competences** that make the development of personal resources possible in order to integrate them into the environment with a spirit of service aimed at "being there for the others";
2. **values** such as personal and social development and ethical commitment;
3. essential learning **attitudes** such as autonomy, students' personal responsibility for their own learning process and cooperation;

4. **Learning** like the development of the learning context, personal reflection, the incorporation of knowledge and its practical application and the critical assessment of the whole process.

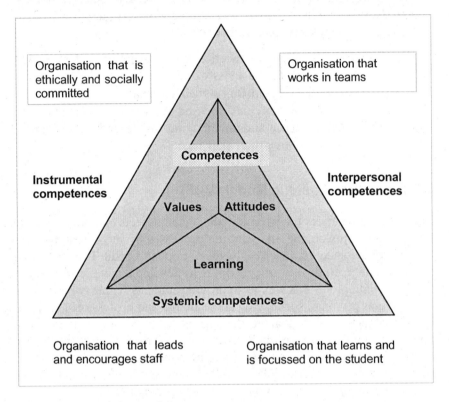

Fig. 2. Deusto training model

The development of specific learning attitudes such as autonomy, the students' personal responsibility for their own learning process and cooperation, the acquisition of values in accordance with the UD's mission, are of utmost importance in this approach. The learning model is intended for personal and social development, ethical commitment and an open attitude to transcendence. The implementation of the MDF is based on a management system which organises, plans, develops and assesses university activities.

A team at the Department of Education at the UD has been involved in the creation and in the drafting of the MDF under the supervision of the Vice Rector for Innovation and Quality.

Both the Strategic Plan and the MDF are currently promoted and supported as much as possible by any means of communication so that the internal staff, students, teaching and administrative staff as well the external world can get to know them.

3.6 Design and planning process of teaching and learning activities

The evaluation process at the UD is part of the MDF involving all projects concerning academic life aspects. The first faculty involved in the process was Economics (both in Bilbao and in San Sebastian). By the end of 2005 all faculties (8) will be involved in the MDF. The MDF is a very complex and detailed project that is divided into several projects or sub-processes such as the 'teaching staff collegiality process', the design and planning process of teaching and learning activities, learning management, assessment, review and improvement processes. Each one can be further split up into sub-processes. Every degree should set out sub-processes in detail.

By way of example, the following list describes all the necessary steps for the design of teaching and learning activities and the relative planning sub-process:

1. write s detailed description of the subject (module) related to the academic-professional profile, the European Credits Transfer System (ECTS) and the MDF;
2. describe learning outcomes in terms of competences to be achieved;
3. develop learning units structure;
4. select contents and competences for each learning unit;
5. promote, develop and incorporate the values which are indicated in the curriculum (i.e. contents, practices, debates, etc.);
6. implement the Deusto Educational Model and draw up the student's autonomous learning guide with particular reference to objectives, contents, activities, work systems (contact hours, seminars, workshops and/or individual work);
7. define how ICTs should be used;
8. estimate students' workload in terms of number of hours and perform the necessary adjustments according to the number of credits (ECTS) allocated to the module;
9. define follow-up and feedback systems for students' work provided for by the module;
10. implement a tutorial system for students' individual and teamwork supervision, including timetables;
11. draw up a learning guide to be handed out to students;

12. select and design didactic materials and resources;
13. select ITC resources such as access to computers, databases, electronic magazines, platforms, etc;
14. draw up a bibliography;
15. supply orientation and writing guidelines for the drafting of students' papers (compulsory, optional, in-depth studies);
16. set up a learning assessment system.

3.7 Internal evaluation process at the Universidad de Deusto - the Technical Unit for innovation and quality (UTIC)

The Technical Unity for Innovation and Quality (UTIC - Unidad Técnica de Innovación y Calidad) is the internal quality unit of the UD and it includes 1 full-time director, 3 part-time professors and 1 scholar.

The UTIC'S mission is to support faculties and units in re-planning and re-engineering their teaching processes and internal organisation within a quality system. Furthermore, the UTIC supplies financial as well as human resources for technological development and logistical adjustments. Its mission is to raise awareness about quality and the precise and strict controls concerning the assessment of processes and outcomes. The following activities are carried out to this purpose:

– set up an internal quality assurance system in all faculties, units and centres of the UD;
– support the implementation of and compliance with standards;
– work out the indicators and the standards of the internal quality assurance and to support their implementation at the UD;
– gather data to compare the objectives met by one faculty/unit with other faculties/units;
– plan research activities and studies to back the analysis of the students' learning paths and to assess their progress and evolution;
– plan quality tools for satisfaction assessment;
– regularly publish the objectives achieved;
– design a database including specific and common quality elements among different units and faculties.

The UTIC'S support to units and faculties is of utmost importance to improve their internal organisation and, at the same time, to carry out internal quality management processes. Professors' assessment and improvement, teaching processes assessment, students' learning and work activities, the use of ITCs and the development of teaching programmes are some of the projects carried out by the UTIC staff.

The Quality commission, which includes six members, is also part of the UTIC and it revises the approved projects and supervises the standards' feasibility, benefits and implementation. Moreover, the commission suggests changes, puts forward solutions for gaps and errors, submits new initiatives in line with the European standards to the Governing boards and sets new quality management actions.

3.8 Label ECTS Docente Project

The Label ECTS Docente project is part of the main objectives of the UTIC and it will be implemented in September 2005, when the new academic year starts. In the previous months professors will be trained (200 hour-training) in order to get as much information as possible about the project and its implementation. Professors are supplied with guidelines and documentation on evaluation.

All professors in charge of a course are expected to obtain the ECTS Label in compliance with the indicators and the standards established by the Quality Commission as regards the degree course. Such indicators provide information about the achievement of degrees, cross competences and specific competences to be developed and the consequent necessary adjustments of the MDF.

This internal process entails two consistent stages: planning and fulfilment. As regards the planning of the teaching course, professors are required to provide the following indications:

1. results in terms of competence;
2. specific features of scientific contents;
3. students' practice and activities;
4. distribution of the estimated workload;
5. individual and group activities;
6. methods used;
7. students' learning guide;
8. adjustments of the MDF.

Moreover, it is important that professors include tutorial activities in their courses providing students with individual and group counselling, self-learning guidance, feedback work and exercises.

Finally, professors are required to set up a students' evaluation system in compliance with key-indicators such as the level of assistance required, involvement, knowledge of contents, originality, initiative and communication skills. Furthermore, contents have to be expressed in terms of theoretical knowledge; general and specific competences and communication skills should be applied to produce individual/group and oral/written reports, even in virtual forums.

Furthermore, professors are required to report the achievement rate with respect to the objectives set out in the plan and the success rate too. At this point the plan and its fulfilment will be assessed not only by students, who will be asked to fill in a questionnaire, but also by the Department's Board of Directors (Direccion Departemento).

4 Conclusion

The objective of this paper was to present the Quality Assurance policies implemented by the University of Deusto. The following final conclusions can be drawn from this case study. The University of Deusto is a rather small Higher Education Institution with its 16,000 students, more than 2,000 professors and 8 faculties. Consequently, the opportunity to timely monitor facilities, quality assurance processes and stakeholders is partially facilitating the Quality Assurance system implementation and management.

In addition, the UD has placed high premium on students and on their human and professional growth. Quality Assurance stills allows to foster students' cooperation according to their capabilities and responsibilities.

This open minded attitude is not restricted to the internal organisation; the UD plays an active role at international level as well. It has been the first University to have adopted the ECTS label system. Moreover, it currently coordinates the Tuning Projects, whose purpose is to foster European cooperation to develop high-quality, effective and transparent European higher education.

The initial resistance to change shown by a few university members has been gradually replaced by the strong belief that the implementation of a Quality Assurance system represents a fundamental strategic action line.

Aspects of evaluation and accreditation in higher education in France

Pierre Batteau

Université Paul Cézanne at Aix-Marseille, France

1 Some theoretical considerations about accreditation

According to a standard definition, accreditation is "a formal published statement regarding the quality of an institution or a programme following a cyclical evaluation based on agreed standards". Albeit quite precise about the subject of this text, this definition does not tell much about the reasons why accreditation exists and why the issue has become paramount in higher education. Before entering into specific considerations about the French systems of accreditation, it is useful to present a few theoretical considerations.

A large number of research activities in economics has been devoted to the study of trade and exchange in the context of information asymmetry in the last three decades and George Akerlof was awarded a Nobel Prize for proving that competitive free markets cannot operate efficiently when there is information asymmetry as regards the quality of the goods traded - the sellers owning generally better information than the buyers. This result, of course, is to be considered as a challenge for the welfare properties of competitive systems, as stated by the neo-classical economic theory.

Among the types of commodities that show strong information asymmetry, educational services are paramount.

Firstly, education is a service whereby, unlike most goods, production and consumption are not separable. As a result, the value acquired through an educational programme cannot be properly assessed by the receiver. By definition, if somebody wants to learn a new subject, he/she is unable to assess the ex-ante value of a content she is ignorant about.

Secondly, education is a service which is subject to many externalities, which hinder competitiveness. One interesting externality is the value that a business attaches to its special clients, with respect to standard clients. The same applies to classrooms: the standard students will feel that the value of the classroom they are part of is higher if some of the top students of the country, rather than plain students, are part of the same classroom.

The main hindrance to a proper competitive system in the field of higher education is the *adverse selection* risk. Let us now imagine a situation whereby some potential providers of an educational service, e.g. business schools, are offering MBAs programmes on a free competitive market. Each school will contend that its programme is one of the best and that it only selects the best students. When deciding about which schools to apply to, prospective students will take into account the possibility that this statement is untrue and the price he/she will be ready to pay will reflect both his/her hopes and his/her doubts. This compromise price is higher than the price he/she would pay, provided that the quality is poor, and higher than the price he/she would be willing to pay, provided that the quality level is high. Consequently, this price is a strong incentive for both low quality education providers and high quality providers to step out of the market. Balance on the free market can only be achieved through low quality at the lowest price. This is Akerlof's theory in a nutshell.

Conversely, the adverse selection risk represents a hindrance for educational institutions when they strive to attract good students. Assessing the value of a student can be very difficult. Looking at previous academic records can be useful but one should also make sure that the institutions which have granted the student's past degrees are of a suitable quality level. In some disciplines, previous records are less important than the specific results achieved by a student during a particular entrance test or examination especially designed for candidate selection (e.g. the GMAT test for management studies). It is even more difficult to assess the value of applicants when the reference criterion is, for instance, business experience. The selection might turn out to be an "adverse selection": the institution is not particularly interested in candidates, who are accidentally the most enthusiastic candidates, while the targeted profiles do not show up. One could give many examples of new programmes, launched with intensive advertising, which have not taken off and eventually failed because risk had been inadequately managed.

Whenever the risk of information asymmetry and the negative effects from externalities are too severe, education cannot operate in a free competitive system. As a result, education is not governed by free markets in most countries.

More precisely, at the level of primary and high school education, externalities are so strong that education is not left at the parents' decision (e.g. education is compulsory in France until 16). Education is generally provided by a public system. Whenever private institutions are involved, they are not independent from the dominant public system, they are strongly regulated and, in general, highly subsidised.

At the intermediate level of college and university education, there are mixed situations according to whether countries are public-oriented or private-oriented. But even in this case, the governance system of such institutions and their regulations are not precisely governed by the free market (e.g. the trustees in US institutions). Even in the US, the effects of adverse selection are so subtle and sophisticated that a system of profit-oriented private institutions competing for market shares is not conceivable. Some authors, however, contend that such a system would lead to greater efficiency and less waste of resources than the present situation.

At the same time adult education, which should grow at a high rate in the next decades, is often left to free market economics whereby mechanisms are required to counter the negative effects of information asymmetry. In executive education, for instance, business schools are competing with powerful consulting companies in the US as well as everywhere in Europe.

Since information asymmetry is an important feature of the economics of education, high premium must be placed on information processes.

It is once again worth presenting some theoretical propositions. In order to restore efficiency, agents must implement strategies which prevent adverse selection. One strategy extensively studied by the literature is «signalling». One of the pioneers of the economic theory of signalling is Michael Spence who has also been awarded the Nobel Prize.

Signalling is basically an action which is undertaken by informed people to foster uninformed people to trust the good quality of the services they provide. In order for this process to be successful, the cost of the action should be as varied as possible so that discrimination arises. Providers of good quality services are interested in this action while providers of low quality services are not. The latter are either compelled to stay on the market or to provide their services at a lower price since the quality of their services has been revealed. Many signalling devices have been identified in real economic and business situations. Some are quite natural, such as the guarantees given, for instance, as regards the market of used cars, but others are more subtle. Some e-banking pioneers were not successful because they had forgotten that brick-and-mortar, in particular when it is adorned with gold, marbles and masterpiece paintings, is important to signal the customers that the bank has massively invested to stay long enough in the market to produce significant returns on its customers savings.

When the market offers a range of providers with a great variety of different quality levels, a very efficient signalling device is reputation. A competitor can imitate an innovation in a short span of time but cannot do the same with reputation. Reputation is long and costly to acquire. However, it can be destroyed rapidly. The signalling effect operates since the uninformed party is aware of it and anticipates that a reputed provider cannot take the risk of endangering its reputation. Reputation creates trust and allows for a higher price.

However, reputation becomes less efficient as a signalling device when the environment changes very rapidly since it takes quite a while to build it. The people who have newly entered an emerging technology sector do not have enough time to build up reputation and must find other signalling mechanisms. The same applies to established sectors whereby the number of providers is rapidly growing as result, for instance, of deregulation, or of a change in the demand.

Accrediting mechanisms can replace reputation. An accrediting mechanism delivers information about the content of the services provided. However, this is not the most relevant aspect, since the uniformed party usually does not know accreditation reports in detail. But achieving accreditation is a way to induce the uninformed party to trust the provider who has been able to be taken into consideration by a recognised independent body and achieve an acknowledgment that others cannot obtain. Consequently, loosing accreditation, after having enjoyed it for a given period of time, is disastrous for the provider. This represents a guarantee for the uninformed buyer that the provider will not endanger its accreditation.

If we then considered employees as the providers (of their skills), the uninformed parties would be the employers and classical examples of accreditation would be diplomas. Diplomas have actually been extensively studied as signalling devices in the literature. For instance, without a recognised degree, medical consulting would be subject to a severe adverse selection risk. Since most people know little about medical sciences, anybody could virtually introduce himself/herself as a doctor and nobody would be interested in asking further information.

When companies are the providers, accreditation is represented by ISO certifications. They replace reputation more effectively in sectors where the pace of change is fast and there is a large information asymmetry between buyers and sellers, in particular when quality cannot be ensured by mere inspections but is embedded in the complex processes leading to the production of goods or services.

The case of education is particularly interesting because of the simultaneous presence of the adverse selection risk on both sides of the market: the quality of the institutions is not easily assessed by the students and the quality of the candidate students is not known unless institutions perform costly investigation activities.

Before having a look at the new trends in higher education accreditation in France bearing in mind the theoretical considerations developed here, it is not worth introducing the main features of the French education system.

2 Features and peculiarities of the French system of higher education

The French higher education system of is essentially run by the state under the close supervision of the government. It has been shaped by four centuries of domination of the economic and social activity by the State. However, the system includes two different types of institutions: *universités* and *grandes écoles* (schools). Historical reasons explain this duality. The Colbertist tradition, inspired by the mercantilist doctrine - Colbert was the minister of Louis XIV - has led every government department to organise its own training activities for highly skilled personnel, instead of entrusting training to universities or external institutions. Today, many *écoles* are operating under the shared authority of the Ministry of Education and another Ministry. For instance, the *Ecole Polytechnique* is a military school, the *Ecole des Mines* is affiliated with the Ministry of Industry and the *Ecole des Ponts et Chaussées* is part of the Ministry of public infrastructures, which is called *Equipement.* The Ministry of Agriculture has its own *écoles.* However, there are many *écoles* which are under the sole authority of the Ministry of Education and these were generally set up in the last two or three decades. For two centuries the *Université*, which is generally referred to as a singular word in French, largely invested in the training of teachers and researchers and showed little consideration for the needs of the economy and companies. Only two disciplines - Law and Medical Sciences - were treated differently, since they were preparing the traditional "professionals": doctors and lawyers (*avocats*).

The modern university system has been set up in 1968 with the creation of about seventy autonomous universities. The outlines of these universities have been defined after an intense debate within the academic community. The most radical positions were in favour of abolishing the *grandes écoles* and integrating them within the universities. Such a position has been defended again in 1984 when the socialist government passed a new law to revise the 1968 law. But the resistance of the schools and the alumni associations has allowed the *écoles* to survive and eventually to thrive, even under the socialist government which created a few new ones. The average funding per student is proportional to the level of prestige of the school. Therefore, less selective university departments receive the lowest funding.

At the same time, the resistance to the idea of autonomous universities has always been widespread within the academic community. Nowadays, the official title of a professor is *professeur des universités* and not *professeur à l'université de...* to recall that a *professeur,* although attached to a particular university, has been appointed at a national level and can exert his/her function in any university. This has produced a mixed system in which universities enjoy certain autonomy in their resource allocation and diploma policies but have almost no leeway in their human resources policy, since academic and administrative staff are appointed and evaluated by national procedures.

The reason of this resistance to autonomy lies in the traditional bias against competition, which is widespread in the French opinion. In the collective mind and following Colbert's theories, France tends to consider itself as a single company competing against other nations. Internal competition is therefore not welcome at university level as well as in the case of large companies. As a result, competition is fierce among very young students since entering a prestigious *"école"* or an excellent university department is subject to intense competition. There are today almost hundred public *universités*. They welcome about 1,300,000 students. During the last thirty-five years about thirty new universities have been created, often in smaller cities. There are different types of *écoles* offering variable length courses. Here we are interested mainly in the *"grandes écoles"*, which are broken down under two categories: the *grandes écoles d'ingénieurs*, which are mainly public institutions and welcome less that 50,000 students. The studies last three years after a two/three year preparation in special sections of the secondary system called *classes préparatoires*.

Most of the *grandes écoles de commerce et de management* control the chambers of commerce – they are therefore called *écoles consulaires* – welcome about 50,000 students. This system is actually very similar to the public system for two reasons. Firstly, although chambers of commerce are managed by the elected representatives of the business world, they are strongly regulated by the State, since they act as tax receiver in many instances, and, in particular, in their educational function. Secondly, their degrees and diplomas receive a form of accreditation by the Ministry of Education.

There is also a tiny group of prestigious schools, which are specific and do not fall in either category, including the *Ecole Normale Supérieure*, which trains professors and researchers and the *Ecole Normale d'Administration*, which trains higher civil servants.

There are many differences between the *universités* and the *grandes écoles* systems. We will focus on two of them: the governance and the recruitment of students. Three elected boards govern universities; one is responsible for administration, one for research and the other one for students' life. The university president – *le president* – must be a member of the faculty and is elected for five years by a college made up by the members of the three boards (roughly 120 people). On the contrary, a *directeur* managing a *grande école* is appointed by the ministry. The board is made up of appointed members and the president of the board is not a member of the permanent staff.

The second distinguishing feature is the student recruitment in the early periods. Selection is performed for the *écoles*, but there is no selection for the *universités*. Actually, selection does exist in some universities, in particular in the *Instituts Universitaires de Technologie (IUT)*, which were set up in 1965 and welcome about 100,000 undergraduate students. The IUT are universities but they look more like *an école* since they are autonomous bodies with a separate budget and allocation of funds. They select students and their director is appointed and not elected. We will not take them into consideration here since we are focusing more on graduate studies rather than on undergraduate studies.

Students can freely enter any university and, apart from a few specific cases, they never meet any selection barrier before entering the fifth year of university. Every year final exams only determine the right to have access to the higher level. Universities are therefore forced to provide a higher education public service on a large scale, which drains away a great deal of their resources. Since students are formally well represented in the university boards and participate in the election of the president, the governance of the universities is aimed at the achievement of this public service.

On the contrary, entering a school generally requires a first selection for a two-year programme (*classe préparatoire*) and then a further selection is performed trough an entrance examination to a school. The *grandes écoles* are ranked according to a prestige hierarchy, which is old and highly determined by the attitudes of the students themselves. By way of example, students who want to enter a school of management also have to pass a national examination on the same day and are ranked at national level. They choose a school according to their results and their choice reflects the hierarchy of the schools. The school then selects the best students among those who have not been selected by a school of higher status. In the last fifty years this hierarchy has practically remained unchanged at the top. Similarly, in engineering disciplines, a very small set of school, which are all located in Paris, enrol the best students coming from the *classes préparatoires*. Surprisingly enough, every year it is possible to see students entering a school as prestigious as the *Ecole des Ponts et Chaussées* who feel intense frustration because they have failed to be admitted to the school of higher status, the *Ecole Polytechnique*. Their behaviour is justified since this hierarchy will have an impact on their whole life of graduates. If they embark on a career in the public administration or in state-owned companies, this hierarchy will be preserved. Most private large companies also feature a hierarchal organisation which reflects public administration. It is not by chance that many French CEOs have worked several years as civil servants before moving to the private sector. Moreover, the agreements passed at the national level for the sector, which are called *conventions collectives*, formally divide schools and diplomas in categories according to jobs and career parameters, such as salary, promotion rules, and pension schemes.

For these reasons, the hierarchy of quality and attractiveness of the French *grandes écoles* proved to be very stable during several decades. It is clear that – according to the definition previously mentioned – such a system has made accreditation relatively useless in the last decades. The *grandes écoles* had no proper signalling strategies. The choice of the students played a pivot role and a fixed hierarchy determined the quality of the institutions. The *grandes écoles* were not competing among themselves: they were letting the students compete for them. The rank implicitly assigned to the school by the established hierarchy would thwart any effort to increase quality and offer better career prospects to its graduates. Why should they have made such an effort since the school alumni would never move from category B to category A, in the law or in the *conventions collectives*?

However, competition among the *grandes écoles de commerce* has recently become fiercer. This is due to the fact that universities have seen a decrease in their number of students since they started to offer programmes which are similar to those provided by the *grandes écoles*. Since universities charge comparatively low fees, they have become less attractive. According to the theoretical propositions, when competition increases in services which are subject to adverse selection, the need for a signalling device is stronger.

3 The French accreditation systems and their evolution

There are several accreditation systems in France and a distinction has to be made between *grandes écoles* and *universités* because of the different nature of competition.

3.1 Accreditation of schools

Because of previously mentioned reasons, the accreditation of schools has not been considered as a crucial issue over the years. Of course, accreditation procedures existed, but they were used only for new schools or degrees and only too rarely for the established ones. For instance, the *grandes écoles d'ingénieurs* grant a diploma awarding the title of *ingénieur diplomé*. This diploma opens the door to attractive careers in French companies and in the public sector. The title is awarded under the supervision of a national committee called *"Commission du Titre d'Ingénieur"* which was established in 1934 in order to protect the title and to prevent its dissemination without control. For years this committee had mainly dealt with the new applications for admission to the club of *grandes écoles d'ingénieurs*, but has almost never discussed about the schools already in the club. A few years ago, for instance, it was found out that schools that no longer existed still enjoyed accreditation. Recently, the role and the procedures of the commission have been redefined to embrace the modern approach to accreditation.

For the *grandes écoles de commerce* there used to be only a simple and formal recognition procedure carried out by the State which was called *visa*. Once the *visa* was granted, it was rarely withdrawn. Here again, the quite stable hierarchy of schools was a sufficient piece of information for candidates, students and employers. A new procedure has recently been introduced. The case is interesting because it illustrates some of the most recent trends in the evolution of the French system.

Shortly after the Sorbonne declaration in June 1998, in the run-up to the Bologna meeting, the French socialist Minister of Education, Claude Allègre, who is a well-known scientist specialised in earth sciences, started to rock the boat and proposed a reform with new accreditation procedures which were more suitable to the increasing competition at European and national level.

Since the readability of the French old diplomas, called *Maîtrise* and *DESS* was too weak, the Ministry introduced a new degree called *master* – an English word now recognised as French – covering all degrees achieved after five years of university studies. However, this prompted *grandes écoles*, which award their degrees after five years, to ask for the permission to name their own diploma *master*. Given the difficulty to assimilate a specific university degree which was accredited on the basis of its contents, with a school programme leading to a professional degree, the Ministry made a subtle distinction between the *master* regarded as a *diplôme* and the *master* regarded as a *grade*. The former rewarded successful completion of a two-year university programme, whereas the latter simply identified the level of the degree the school. So institutions external to the universities were authorised to award the university *master* qualification.

Clearly, this distinction has not been completely assimilated by the French and, a fortiori, by the foreigners yet, but it has determined a complete reshaping of accreditation within the *grandes écoles*. The *grandes écoles* d'ingénieurs, which were state-run and were subject to the authority of the *Commission du Titre d'Ingénieur(CTI)* have been automatically authorised to award the *grade de master* along with their degrees after five years of studies, which included two years of *classes préparatoires* outside the school and three years within the school. The CTI itself has been re-vamped.

The situation was different for the *grandes écoles de commerce* since they were administered by the chambers of commerce or were purely pri-vate. Stakeholders started to think that the *grandes écoles de commerce* asking for the recognition of their degree as a *grade* de *master* should not be subject to an evaluation procedure.

The government appointed a task force to draft the decree for the new procedure. The intention of the Ministry, as declared by the highest official (*Directeur des Enseignements Supérieurs*) at the first meeting, was to test a new evaluation procedure. This would provide a model which could be later extended to all *université* degrees of the management and commerce field. It is apparent that the most attractive schools the procedure was ad-dressed to had already been accredited at an international level by means of the EQUIS procedure, which was initiated by an association of Euro-pean business schools (EFMD for European Foundation for Management Development). This was due to the need for signalling devices on the part of the most attractive schools, which wanted to meet rising competition and thus conquer students.

The EQUIS model has exerted a profound influence on the talks of the task force. Moreover, the new procedure implemented by the *Commission du Titre d'Ingénieur* also provided a model and common meetings have been organised with *Commission*'s members. A few months later in 2001 a national commission, which was called *Commission d'Evaluation des Formations et Diplômes de Gestion*, was officially set up. This commis-sion included representatives of universities, chambers of commerce and government branches involved in management and commerce. However, this was the first time that an institution awarding university grades had in-cluded only a minority of members from the University. Of course, the de-cision was criticised by the stakeholders who wanted to preserve the mo-nopoly of universities over the diplomas as far as possible, but the first years of activity of the commission have gone smoothly and today its role seems to be recognised and accepted.

From a practical viewpoint, the commission appoints two experts – one of them must necessarily be a university representative – who have to visit the school and inquire about the specific degree for which accreditation is applied. They draw up a report which is submitted to the school for possible objections and then put forward to the commission, which makes the final decision. Accreditation is granted for a limited period of time, five years in general, although shorter conditional accreditation has been granted in special cases. Most schools have accepted to go before the commission to be authorised to award the *grade de master*. INSEAD, a private institution belonging to the tiny group of top global business schools has even applied for recognition of its MBA as a French *master*.

3.2 Accreditation of university programmes

In the case of universities, evolution started in the seventies when universities were faced with an increasing market demand for more specialised and better skilled staff. Until the mid seventies, the main task of universities was the education of the next generation of secondary school teachers (for *lycées* and *colleges*) and public researchers. The performance of their students in the national contests (*concours*) for teachers' recruitment in the secondary school system and research field provided an evaluation of the quality of universities.

In the mid-seventies a large number of students started to enrol at university since no entrance examinations were sat. The majority of university age people decided to go to university. To avoid rejecting too many students after two years given the limited number of jobs in public education and research, universities launched professional degrees for careers in other remaining fields of society. The issue of quality evaluation was then brought to the forefront. Any university offers two types of degrees: the "*diplômes d'Etat*" and the *diplômes d'université*. The latter remain a prerogative of universities and the only indication of quality is provided either by market recognition or by good media assessment. The *diplômes d'université* do not receive any state funding. On the contrary, the *diplômes d'Etat* must be accredited by a national body – the French word is *habilitation* – and are consequently state funded.

To perform this type of accreditation, the French Ministry has tested the implementation of several systems. However, the basic idea has always been peer evaluation. The evaluators, who are called *experts*, are selected by the Ministry in each discipline. The French academic world is divided into 77 scientific disciplines and each discipline is managed by a national committee, which is in charge of the appointment and promotion of university professors. The criterion of competence and academic recognition prevails, but the members chosen generally share a common vision of the university with the incumbent Minister and his/her staff, and have sometimes affiliations with the political party in office.

The national evaluators examine the project of running a *diplôme d'Etat* course. The outcome depends on the discipline and the personality of the evaluators and the Minister. There is an old tradition in the French University for university courses. On the contrary, university lectures cannot be monitored. By definition, a university professor is supposed to be at the cutting edge of his discipline and must teach students the latest discoveries and recent ideas. In the secondary system supervision is performed by a body of auditors who are independent from teachers (the *inspecteurs*). On the contrary, the contents of university courses cannot be subject to external inspection. This extreme position is in conflict with the need for accreditation when universities deliver professional degrees. The only viable possibility is therefore peer evaluation.

Some evaluators admit that their peer colleagues can bring about innovation and new pedagogical methods and contents. They firmly stick to the principle of academic independence. Consequently, they just check that the candidate degree meets a set of basic requirements (e.g. is the faculty striking a good balance between academics and practitioners? Do the targeted jobs really exist in the economy?).

In other cases, the Minister and the appointed evaluators have a common opinion of the discipline and of the corresponding degrees. They have in mind a curriculum model for all university programmes leading to a specified degree. They expect each candidate programme to comply with the model. In this case the university autonomy is reduced. In recent years many academic members have complained that their status becomes closer to that of the teachers in the secondary school system: they are supposed to deliver knowledge according to nationally defined programmes and rules and their freedom of choice is shrinking. The reality features more indistinct outlines and probably follows the Lawrence and Lorsch "differentiation-integration" model. The system is not actually hostile to innovation and those who want to practice it, find relatively supportive evaluators. The large number of new degrees created in the last five years, and in particular during the LMD shift in the last two years, is evidence of the willingness of innovation. Nevertheless, once innovation is implemented, the pressure for common standards, which are expected by the students, the media and the employers, restores the government's role as the "great integrator". Efforts are then made to manage the excessive variety brought about by innovation. This is a traditional way of functioning whenever a market system cannot operate selection and sort out positive and negative innovations.

Although the scenario is more complex, one can observe that evaluators of first type tend to belong to the group of academics who think that there is not enough competition in the French system. They therefore favour local innovation and differentiation. The extreme positions would favour very autonomous universities with freedom in faculty recruitment and customised contracts in an environment of fierce competition, which means student selection and probably entrance fees.

The evaluators of second type want as little competition as possible among the universities and deem that there is too much variety in the supply. They want to preserve a centralised state control over the diplomas and prefer to slow down differentiation. Their view is influenced by the fears of increasing privatisation of French universities or by the fact that they believe that university professors will lose the civil servant status.

In practice, the difference lies with the issue of balance between cooperation and competition among universities. It should be noted that political attitudes do not explain the inclination towards innovation-competition versus integration-state control. A part of the rightists embrace the liberal philosophy favouring competition while another larger part sticks to the Colbertist tradition of the dominance of the State. Those who are left-oriented and aware of the weaknesses of France in the international academic competition arena are favourable to more competitive market conditions. They are in conflict with the larger part of the left that sees variety and autonomy as a liberal dream hiding a likely dismantling of the celebrated French public services. The vote on the European constitution project in May 2005 has triggered an intense debate in the country about these notions and it has become clear that the issue deeply divides both the Left and the Right.

No formal visit is generally scheduled for the evaluation and evaluators focus exclusively on the project. When re-accreditation is applied for, the file must include a report about the past period containing general statistics about the programme, career paths of alumni and resources consumed. For new projects with a professional orientation, detailed description is required and it should be proved that actual career opportunities are available by means of a letter written by potential employers or experts of the sector supporting the project.

For projects with a "research orientation", other additional requirements about the research environment in which the project takes place must be met. For instance, a university which wants to offer a "research master" degree course in biology, can do so only if there is a locally recognised research centre in the discipline, if there is a local body of researchers willing to teach and supervise the activities of students and if the programme is closely linked to this centre.

The outcome of the evaluation can be threefold: acceptance, rejection, or "*navette*" (shuttle), which implies a back and forth dialogue between the evaluators and the university. Most *navettes* end up with acceptance. The *navette* allows for possible improvements. Quite often, it is triggered by the fact that a university or other universities in the neighbourhood have proposed similar degrees. Since the Ministry is committed to funding the accepted programmes, there is a strong pressure for grouping similar demands into the same project.

Initiatives for a new programme cannot be launched at any time. For receiving the necessary resources, universities generally have a four year planning (*plan quadriennal*) with possible half term revision. The evaluation cycles tend now to be consistent with this planning. Accreditation is usually given for four years and a new evaluation occurs at the end of the term. The fact that the same evaluators work at the same time on the overall set of similar degrees in the country, makes it possible to implement a national policy of "diplomas map". This favours consistency in terms of supply and a good use of public funds, but it often limits the claimed autonomy of universities and may slow down innovations.

Doctorates are a special case. They represent the core of university activities and the only level at which they have a quasi-monopoly. A special institution called *école doctorale* (*ED*) runs doctoral programmes. An *ED* is not formally an independent organisation and is necessarily a division of an existing university. However, when many universities are located in the same area, such as a city or a cluster of cities, and operate within the same group of disciplines, the Ministry issues accreditation for a single *ED*. *EDs* are often lateral organisations and for this reason have some degree of freedom with respect to the parent university.

It should also be noted that whenever a *grande école* wishes to launch a programme for a degree usually granted by universities, such as a research-oriented *master*, the same procedure implemented by universities applies. Conversely, if a university sets up its own "*école d'ingénieurs*", the *Commission du Titre d'Ingénieur* evaluates the project.

Finally, it should be mentioned that a national body supervises all the activities of universities. This committee, which is called *CNESER* (*Conseil National de l'Enseignement Supérieur et de la Recherche*) is composed of 61 elected members, representing all higher education stakeholders (professors, administrative and technical staff, researchers, and students). The CNESER votes on any accreditation before the decision is taken by the Ministry. The election of the *CNESER* is definitely politically-oriented and generally leads to an over-representation of the left and the extreme left among the students and staff representatives. For this reason, it is likely that the *CNESER* will not enthusiastically welcome accreditation procedures leaning more towards competition and the signalling of excellence. In some instances, the *CNESER* and the *Commission d'Evaluation des Enseignements de Gestion* have disagreed on issues that are central to accreditation. For instance, the issue of selection is often controversial, since it is a common feature of *grandes écoles*, but a forbidden concept for many members of the *CNESER*.

3.3 Other evaluation procedures

There are other evaluation procedures implemented in the French system. As previously mentioned, French universities are part of a public system and are under the authority of the central government. In this respect, the evaluation processes described above are internal. People who have a direct interest in the system manage processes. They are often in charge of degrees themselves which are in direct competition with the degrees they have to evaluate. To provide an external assessment of the performance and the quality of French universities, the Parliament has voted in the early eighties for the creation of a national committee (*Comité National d'Evaluation*) which is independent of the universities and the Ministry. The President appoints this committee. Each university is evaluated every four or five years and the report is published. From a practical viewpoint, the committee sends a delegation of auditors to visit the university and meet faculty staff, and students. The operation can last several days because of the number of people involved and the facilities to visit. Many French universities have facilities scattered over several locations. This type of evaluation is general and descriptive, but it is useful as a first approach to appraise the strengths and weaknesses of a particular university. The Ministry offices often refer to this document when they negotiate with a university for preparing the four-year planning or for bargaining over slots and budgets. There is no accreditation after this audit.

4 Perspectives, problems and trends

The previous description explains that accreditation plays two distinct roles:

According to the theory, when competition increases in this type of service, the need for signalling mechanisms becomes more compelling. The demand for accreditation increases and this has been the case in the most competitive areas, such as management, commerce and business education. Accreditation mitigates the risk of adverse selection, upholds the price, if any, and promotes the image of the institutions when they compete for students on the market.

Accreditation plays another role when, as previously mentioned, the Ministry in charge of the strategic orientations and budget allocation tends to view universities as subordinated entities and does not regard competition as a primary objective among them. Cooperation is the main concern. Accreditation – *habilitation* in the French – entails internal auditing procedures which shed some light on the local activities carried out to allocate resources adequately. They also serve the purpose of informing potential partners about cooperative activities. Partners can get to know the real situation of the applying institution. In fact, networks involving university departments in various disciplines tend to aggregate institutions with similar *habilitations*. The *habilitation* process most probably looks different in both cases because one or the other of its functions needs to be emphasised.

However, new events and circumstances could lead to a change in the Ministry procedures. A big change has occurred since 2003 in the French university system to make its degrees more compliant with the Bologna agreement.

Traditionally, university studies were broken down under three different stages: the undergraduate stage called *premier cycle,* lasting two years, the *licence* and *maîtrise* stage (one year each), called *second cycle* and the *troisième cycle*, a stage which was divided into several categories of degrees, such as the *Diplôme d'Etudes Supérieurs Spécialisées (DESS)*, which lasted one year and was practice-oriented, the *Diplôme d'Etudes Approfondies (DEA)*, which lasted one year and was research-oriented, and finally the *doctorat*, which lasted between 3 and 5 years.

University studies are now divided into three stages: Licence (three years), Master (two more years) and Doctorate (three more years), hence the designation LMD or 3-5-8. The peculiarity is that entry to the M period (M1) does not entail any selection, although universities implement a whole series of tricks to select students, whereas entrance to the second year (M2) of the master's degree course entails a selection procedure. This leads to the question of what should be done with the students rejected after one year of master preparation.

However, old degrees have not been suppressed since they are a prerequisite for applying for *concours* for public positions and many private jobs defined by the *conventions collectives*. Moreover, the master's qualification awarded by the *grandes écoles* is not consistent with LMD since they follow a three-year scheme after two years of preparation, while the LMD scheme requires three years (L) before the M period, which lasts two years.

The LMD reform has been considered at first as an opportunity to revamp university degrees and in some universities, this has actually occurred. Obsolete programmes have been closed or merged with new ones; concentration of resources has been achieved, and more readable degree courses description have been made available. However, in many other cases, the proposals put forward have shown a waste of efforts and reflected mere defensive moves to protect vested interests.

The expectation was that accreditation procedures might have played a disciplinary role. However, it seems that the Ministry has eventually accepted a large number of proposals resulting in an excessive dispersion of the education provision. As a result, universities were compelled to run after students to be able to continue running their degree courses. The reason for this apparent *laissez-faire* might be of political nature: the first moves towards LMD in 2003-2004 triggered extremely unfavourable reactions from the students and their parents, who were supported by some teachers' unions. The government has judged that the risks of an entire rejection of the reform were high, and, as a result, hundreds of thousands of students would be put in the streets. The idea was to calm the unrest by showing a positive attitude towards all projects. It should also be noted that experts have had only a short time to examine a huge mass of new projects and only a few tools had been made available. A comprehensive inspection of the facts and the proposals presented in the projects was impossible. The experts preferred the risk of accepting dubious projects rather than rejecting good ones. This example shows that the accreditation system has not worked properly and requires deeper investigation.

However, the pressure for change is increasingly high and it mainly derives from the global trends in higher education. Some years ago, the French media started to publish rankings of the universities, schools, and programmes in terms of performance and quality. The criteria were sometimes questioned. In some cases, for instance, the ranking would judge the efficiency of the process on the basis of the ratio of graduates over newly-enrolled students by showing the drop-out or rejection rate during the studies. The lowest rejection rates were ranked top while the top institutions attracting many students – with no entrance selection but very selective at the end – were ranked at the bottom. The method simply reflected a university logic according to which excellence should not be aimed at; the mail goal was rather bringing as many people as possible at the higher level in the spirit of the *service public*.

The media are now faced with the new challenge of positioning the degrees in the European landscape. The complexity of the French systems has made this task quite uneasy. In the meantime, international mass media have published rankings showing that the French systems are too much focused on domestic needs with little awareness of the increasing competition among universities at a global level.

It is not by chance that the most pro-active attitudes towards accreditation have been shown by institutions in the field of business and management education, where there is an intense international competition for both students' recruitment and their graduates' placements. The first shocks came some years ago when the rankings of European institutions in management education were published by the Financial Times. A school like the HEC (*Ecole des Hautes Etudes Commerciales*), which has been sitting at the top of the domestic pyramid for decades, providing the French business world with countless marketing and sales directors and many CEOs, was confined to a lower position. The French observers immediately complained about an Anglo-Saxon bias of the survey. However, the ranking showed that the school organisation was strictly related to its role as leader of the network of the French *grandes écoles de commerce* and that the school was not so willing to play a major role at European level. For instance, the MBA is the degree that makes such an institution internationally visible. Regardless of all the criticisms concerning the MBA, the international use of the concept and the domination of the great US business schools make it a *passage obligé* for top positions in the rankings. The HEC is running a very good MBA programme, taught mostly in English, with an international audience of students featuring professional experience and the best professors of the HEC enjoy teaching in it. However, the HEC must primarily defend its position of leader in the complex system of recruitment procedures of French students via the *concours d'entrée*. For this reason, the MBA programme, at first, might not have been associated with the name HEC and was developed as a separate entity called ISA (*Institut Supérieur des Affaires*). Today the HEC is striving to impose its MBA and its main competitors are INSEAD, the London Business School, the IMD in Lausanne, the IESE in Barcelona and some others.

A more recent shock, at the scale of the whole system, came with the celebrated ranking of world universities issued by the University of Shangaï. When it was first published at the end of 2003, the effect in France was devastating: this ranking was not based on an American biased criterion, as might have been suspected in the case of MBAs. It simply focused on international visibility of research, faculty and alumni. The first French institution in the list ranked sixty fifth; the two most prestigious *grandes écoles* in France, and *Ecole Normale Supérieure* and *Ecole Polytechnique* were respectively 107th and 253rd. Moreover, besides the majority of US institutions, UK, Sweden, Germany, Switzerland, Canada, Japan, Netherlands and Australia had a representative among the top fifty institutions, but France was not among them.

During the academic year after the publication, many debates have taken place to understand the situation. In the author's university, the president launched a thorough investigation and it turned out that researchers published a large part of their international articles with an improper name of the origin university and that they sometimes used a name dating back to the period prior to the 1968 reform. The reason being that many researchers and professors still see the university as a mere administrative entity. In Paris universities bear numbers and students and even some faculty members sometimes ignore the number of their university. Once again, it should be noted that the concept of autonomous universities has not always been enthusiastically implemented.

The new Shangaï ranking published in 2004 shows the subsequent efforts made and all the French universities which were part of the rank have gained between twenty and thirty ranks. There are now two French representatives in the top 50.

The ranking has essentially raised greater awareness about the importance of an international profile for the French institutions and has focused attention on their rather weak communication policies. It will also probably speed up the improvement process of evaluation procedures in research and, later on, it will have an impact on accreditation procedures by emphasising the importance of international achievements.

However, these adjustments cannot replace a thorough reflection about the effects of an increasing competition in the global higher education scenario. Should the present growth rate in Asia persists for at least some years, the need for European institutions to play a role in higher education in Asian countries will become of vital importance. The nature of competition in this field and the essential effects of information asymmetry will demand more and more sophisticated signalling devices.

How will France react to this challenge? According to the traditional view, a small group of national champions will be pinpointed and receive financial support. A large number of resources will be allocated to them and the others would have to share the cake's leftovers. The UK has applied a similar policy to research, following a deep change in evaluation procedures. In France, recent discussions in the research area were focused on the concept of *pole de compétitivité*. The idea is to devote more attention and allocate more funds to local clusters of universities, research centres, schools and firms to increase their capacity to meet international competition. Evaluation and accreditation procedures will have to be strengthened in order to pinpoint and select the candidates which should receive government financial backing to meet global competition.

Will this trend decrease competition among (and within) universities, by underlining the need for united efforts to fight against foreign competitors?

If so, will the evaluation procedures perform different functions? Far from becoming signalling devices on the domestic market, they would be rather considered as control procedures to serve the purpose of auditing the universities, identifying the most suitable ones to meet global competition in order to allocate most of the resources to them and only a few resources to others. If this turned out to be true, the French institutions (*grandes écoles* or university institutes or departments) which are most subject to international competition will resort more and more to external bodies for finding efficient signalling devices. They will resort to the AACSB (American Association to Advanced Collegiate Schools of Business) or the association of MBA based in the UK. Today getting the EQUIS is more important for an *école de commerce* than the recognition granted by the *commission d'évaluation des formations et diplômes de gestion.*

Printing and Binding: Strauss GmbH, Mörlenbach